Sweet Celebrations

Also by Katherine Kallinis Berman and Sophie Kallinis LaMontagne

The Cupcake Diaries: Recipes and Memories

from the Sisters of Georgetown Cupcake

Sweet Celebrations

Our Favorite Cupcake Recipes, Memories,

and Decorating Secrets

That Add Sparkle to Any Occasion

Katherine Kallinis Berman & Sophie Kallinis LaMontagne

HarperOne

An Imprint of HarperCollinsPublishers

HarperOne

FIRST EDITION

Designed by Jessica Shatan Heslin/Studio Shatan, Inc.

Library of Congress Cataloging-in-Publication Data is available upon request.

ISBN 978–0–06–221036–4

12 13 14 15 16 RRD(C) 10 9 8 7 6 5 4 3 2 1

To Mommy,
who reminds us every day that life is a celebration

ACKNOWLEDGMENTS

Throughout the process of writing this second book, we have been fortunate to enjoy the love and support of many members of our family, friends, and colleagues.

First and foremost, we would like to thank our grandparents, Babee and Papou, for continuing to watch over us and give us strength and inspiration. We think of you every day, and we thank you for teaching us to celebrate life, family, and friends.

To our mother, "Mommy"—you enriched this book with your stories, recipes, and love of all of life's celebrations. You are our best friend and our biggest cheerleader. We would also like to thank our father for his unwavering love and support. We love you both.

To our husbands, Ben Berman and Steve LaMontagne—thank you for always being by our sides along every step of the way. We love you.

To Dayna Smith and Elizabeth Messina—thank you so much for your beautiful photography.

To our wonderful and extremely talented editorial team—Jeanette Perez and Sheryl Berk—it was so much fun to team up again! To Mark Tauber, Claudia Boutote, Suzanne Wickham, Michele Wetherbee, Terri Leonard, Suzanne Quist, Jackie Berkman, and the entire team at HarperCollins and HarperOne—thank you so much for your hard work on this project and for supporting this book.

To Claudia Cross at Folio Literary Management, and Lisa Shotland and Ashley Davis at the Creative Artists Agency—thank you for all your hard work in making this book happen!

To our *DC Cupcakes* "family"—executive producers Doug DePriest, Dan Cesareo, Terence Noonan, and Mark Finkelpearl—thank you for your passion, support, and all your amazing work in bringing our journey to life on screen.

To our extended family at TLC and Discovery Communications—we celebrate this book with all of you, especially David Zaslav, CEO of Discovery Communications; John Hendricks, founder and chairman of Discovery Communications; Eileen O'Neill, group president of Discovery and TLC Networks; Amy Winter, TLC general manager; Howard Lee, TLC SVP of production and development; Alon Orstein, TLC VP of production and development; Caroline Perez, director of development and production; Edward Sabin, Discovery and TLC EVP and group COO; Jennifer Williams, Discovery and TLC SVP of talent management and strategy; Liz Melcher, Discovery and TLC director of talent management and strategy; Laurie Goldberg, Discovery and TLC EVP of communications; Shannon Martin, TLC senior director of communications; Tom Carr, SVP of marketing; Lara Richardson, VP of marketing; Rose Stark, director of marketing; Michelle Theisen, VP of marketing/branded entertainment; Tara Patten, TLC senior director of talent management and strategy; Sue Perez-Jackson, director of licensing; Grant McAllister, manager of licensing; and Cady Burnes, manager of licensing. Thank you for all that you do, and for sharing our story and bringing *DC Cupcakes* to viewers around the world. We are both very proud to be a part of the TLC and Discovery Communications family.

To our staff at Georgetown Cupcake—a special thank you for your hard work, dedication, and passion. Your spirit is what makes Georgetown Cupcake such a special place, and we celebrate this book with all of you.

Finally, to our millions of customers and fans of *DC Cupcakes* all across the world, thank you for letting Georgetown Cupcake be a part of your life celebrations. Celebrations are our life's work, and we hope that the tips and recipes in this book will help you come up with creative ideas for your own celebrations. This book is for you.

Sophie and *Katherine*

CONTENTS

List of Recipes xii

Introduction xvii

PART 1 *LIFE CELEBRATIONS*

Chapter 1: Birthdays 3

Chapter 2: Bridal Showers 21

Chapter 3: Weddings 31

Chapter 4: Anniversaries 49

Chapter 5: Baby Showers 57

PART 2 *HOLIDAYS*

Chapter 6: New Year's Eve 69

Chapter 7: Valentine's Day 79

Chapter 8: Easter 87

Chapter 9: Passover 103

Chapter 10: Mother's Day 109

Chapter 11: Father's Day 119

Chapter 12: Fourth of July 125

Chapter 13: Halloween 131

Chapter 14: Thanksgiving 141

Chapter 15: Christmas 151

Chapter 16: Hanukkah 161

PART 3 *Everyday Parties*

Chapter 17: Sleepovers 171

Chapter 18: Tea Parties 179

Chapter 19: Brunches 189

Chapter 20: Dinner Parties 203

PART 4 *Outdoor Get-togethers*

Chapter 21: Campouts 211

Chapter 22: Pool Parties 219

Chapter 23: Beach Parties 229

Chapter 24: Picnics 237

Chapter 25: Sporting Events 243

PART 5 *DC CUPCAKES' Biggest Bashes*

Chapter 26: Behind the Scenes 251

Cupcake-Decorating Staples 272

Our Favorite Piping Tips 273

Credits 274

Index 275

LIST OF RECIPES
IN *SWEET CELEBRATIONS*

Cupcakes

Almond Easter Bunny Cupcakes 90

American Angel Food Mini Cupcake Flag 128

Anniversary Cupcake Dessert 52

Banana Chocolate Chip Monkey Cupcakes 7

Big Apple Crumble Cupcakes 270

Blackberry Cupcakes with Lemon Filling 182

Blueberry Cheesecake Cupcakes with Blueberry Compote 206

Bridal Shower Lavender Earl Grey Teacake Cupcakes 24

Candy Bar Cupcakes 134

Champagne Cupcakes with Champagne Buttercream and
Fondant Monograms and Roses 38

Cherry Cupcake Tarts 240

Chocolate Peanut Butter Chip Football and Team Jersey Cupcakes 246

Chocolate Salted Caramel Pop Rocks Cupcakes 74

Christmas Ornament Chocolate Eggnog Cupcakes with
Rum Cream Cheese Frosting 154

Citrus Orange or Lime Icy Cupcake Pops 221

Coconut Key Lime Cupcakes with Tropical Umbrellas 232

Cotton Candy Cupcakes Topped with
Cotton Candy–Stuffed Fondant Pillows 174

Cranberry Spice "Turkey" Cupcakes with Vanilla Cream Cheese Frosting 144

Cupcake Flowerpot with Honeybee Yogurt Cupcakes
and Buttercream Frosting 112

Giant Chocolate Hazelnut Cupcake 18

Ginger Peach Cupcakes 192

Greek Walnut Spice Cupcakes 266

"Hamburger" Cupcakes 122

Ice Cream Cone Cupcakes 224

Lemon and Fig Cupcakes 254

Marble Mini Cupcakes 44

Raspberry Buttercream "Tutu" Cupcakes 14

Star of David Blue Velvet Cupcakes 164

Strawberry Shortcake Cupcakes 80

Tie-Dyed Monster Cupcakes 136

Toasted Marshmallow Campfire Cupcakes 214

White Chocolate Mini Egg Cupcakes in Egg Cartons 94

White Chocolate Peppermint Cupcakes 258

Whole Wheat Cranberry Orange Cupcakes 54

Yellow Ducky Cupcakes with Baby Blue and Baby Pink Buttercream Filling 62

TREATS

Caramel- and Chocolate-Drizzled Popcorn 177

Cucumber and Cream Cheese Tea Sandwiches 186

Georgetown Cupcake Chocolate Peppermint Bark 157

Greek Cinnamon Cupcake, Honey, and Yogurt Parfaits 194

Greek Loukoumades (Greek Fritters) 198

Greek Vasilopita (New Year's Cake) 72

Kolokithopita (Greek Pumpkin Phyllo Pastries) 147

Koulourakia (Greek Butter Cookies) 98

Passover Macaroons 106

Strawberry Shortbread Valentine's Cookies 84

Tiganites (Sweet Pancake Medallions) 60

White Cheddar and Marmalade Tea Sandwiches 187

*D*RINKS

Bridal Shower Pink "Mocktails" 28

Old-Fashioned Coke Floats 226

Peach Nectar Iced Tea 197

Sangria 234

Strawberry Milk Shakes 121

Witch's Brew 139

If we had to come up with one word to describe our time as the owners of Georgetown Cupcake, it would be *celebrate*! It's been quite a whirlwind of excitement and parties, from family events like Katherine's wedding to the grand openings of our two new Georgetown Cupcake locations in New York City and Boston and our upcoming store in Los Angeles. And if that wasn't enough, we also set a new Guinness World Record for the world's largest cupcake! A great reason to throw a block party, don't you think? Our first book, *The Cupcake Diaries,* was a bestseller, and we're filming lots more fabulous and fun episodes of our TLC series *DC Cupcakes.* Whew!

Though we always seem to be crazy-busy running all over the place and working at our bakeries day in and day out, we recognize that none of it matters without the people who make our lives so meaningful and joyful. We believe there is a reason to celebrate every single day. For us, celebrating is not just about birthdays and weddings and other big events; it's also about appreciating the little things that make daily life special. Sometimes that can be smelling the aroma of warm cupcakes fresh from the oven, or watching the sun rise at 5:00 A.M. as we are frosting peacefully in the bakery. Other times, it's the beauty of dozens of Red Velvet cupcakes lined up perfectly on a sheet pan, or Mommy bringing us our morning coffee with a smile on her

GEORGETOWN CUPCAKE

face. We vow that no matter how big our business grows—or how many amazing opportunities present themselves—we'll never take things for granted or forget what's important to us.

If you read our first book and watch *DC Cupcakes,* you know that our grandmother Babee was our inspiration for starting Georgetown Cupcake. She's also the person who taught us to celebrate the simple things in life. She instilled in us the belief that each day is a special occasion. We remember how she used her good china daily and always set the table with fresh flowers. She would celebrate each and every one of our small triumphs—whether it was losing a tooth, bringing home a good report card, or winning a tennis match at school—by baking our favorite desserts for us.

When we did have an "official" reason to celebrate, the family parties that Babee threw were legendary. Her preparations started early in the morning: polishing the china and silver, folding the napkins *just so,* setting the table, cutting fresh roses from the bushes on her veranda, and arranging the flowers beautifully in vases. Then, of course, cooking, baking, more cooking, and more baking. As the clock ticked, and there were only minutes to go until the first guests arrived, we helped her plate the food, always family-style. She would garnish each dish with parsley or orange peels, and dust confectioners' sugar on top of her spice cake. She always added these special touches to make her food *shine.* We absolutely loved the excitement of it all: the excitement of *sharing.*

We definitely inherited our love of entertaining from Babee. Now, when our family visits during the holidays, birthdays, or "just because," we go into entertaining overdrive and have so much fun pulling out all the stops for our guests. It may be the Greek in us, but we love to party and throw the biggest and best bashes ever. We want our guests to feel welcome and special. We want to wow them!

This philosophy has transferred over to our professional lives at Georgetown Cupcake. We feel that whenever customers walk through the doors of our bakery, we are welcoming them into our home. We want them to stay awhile and enjoy, not only the delicious cupcakes, but the entire experience. And one of the best perks of owning a bakery is being a part of other people's celebrations. Whenever we get orders for christenings, graduations, engagements, baby showers, anniversaries, or dinner parties, we get so excited. We take great pride in customizing each order and decorating the cupcakes in a way that makes them unique and memorable for our customers. These are the moments that they will always remember, and many times they're the moments we remember as well.

> *We feel that whenever customers walk through the doors of our bakery, we are welcoming them into our home.*

In this second book, we share many more of our best Georgetown Cupcake recipes for cupcakes and other favorite desserts, as well as fun and chic decorating and entertaining how-tos. From creating a sky-high cupcake tower display to laying out a dazzling "do-it-yourself" cupcake topping bar, the possibilities are endless! We'll also share what went on while we were preparing for some of *DC Cupcakes'* biggest celebrations—what you didn't see on screen!

We hope that our baking, decorating, and entertaining secrets will give you the confidence to throw whatever fabulous fete you are dreaming up. And we hope you're inspired to gather with family and friends and just enjoy being together. Make every moment a sweet celebration!

Sophie and *Katherine*

Recipe for Success

Cherish the Little Things

~~~~~~

*W*e loved making these lists; we smile every time we read them. They remind us that you don't need a special occasion to celebrate; just appreciate a moment that is precious because of its beauty, poignancy, or simplicity.

Make a list of your own. Write down those things you cherish most. It can give you a new perspective on how every day can be special and really pick you up when you're feeling stressed or down.

Ten Little Things I Cherish

1. Pink sparkly sanding sugar spilled across the counter . . . looks like fairy dust!

2. Family dinners

3. Perfectly clear blue skies

4. The smell of chocolate melting in a pot on the stove

5. Snow days

6. A bear hug from my husband

7. Old photos of our grandparents

8. Watching the sunrise from our fondant table in the bakery

9. Chocolate Hazelnut cupcakes

10. Snuggling on the couch in my pj's after a long day at the bakery

—*Sophie*

Ten Little Things I Cherish

1. Giving Eskimo kisses to our dog Poochie

2. Eating hot dogs by the pool

3. Smiling, happy customers in our shop

4. Memories of my grandparents

5. Mommy's laugh

6. Carrying lilies of the valley on my wedding day

7. My locket with a picture of my grandparents that I carry everywhere

8. A beautifully packed box of cupcakes

9. The memory of Mommy's eyes filling with tears as I walked down the aisle at my wedding

10. My husband bringing me ice cream in bed

—*Katherine*

Helpful Hints for Baking Through *Sweet Celebrations*

Here are some important tips to keep in mind when baking the recipes in this book:

● **Paper Cupcake Baking Cups vs. Greasing the Pan with Butter** For the vast majority of recipes in this book, we suggest using paper baking cups to bake your cupcakes. If you don't have any on hand, however, you can certainly grease your cupcake pan with butter and do without the baking cups. Try to always use good-quality butter to grease your pans, and never ever use shortening!

● **Types of Baking Cups** At Georgetown Cupcake, we typically use brown paper baking cups for our chocolate cupcakes and white paper baking cups for our vanilla cupcakes. If you are baking a cupcake that you really want to "show off," however, it's best to use the plain white baking cups. When you bake your cupcakes, these cups

will become transparent. If you are baking cupcakes with fresh fruit or candy pieces in the cupcake—or cupcakes that have a beautiful blue batter—a white baking cup will allow your guests to see all of the excitement in the cupcake even before they remove the liner. Patterned or foil baking cups are more suitable for plain vanilla or chocolate cupcakes. When the cupcake itself is one solid color, the patterned liner can help grab your guests' attention.

● **Scraping Down the Bowl** While you're baking your way through the recipes, always remember to stop and scrape down the sides of the bowl if your ingredients start to get caked up.

● **Ingredient Temperature** Unless our recipe specifically states otherwise, make sure that all of your ingredients come to room temperature before baking. This will help ensure that they are well incorporated into the batter and that your cupcakes come out light and fluffy as opposed to dense and bricklike.

● **Choice of Butter** All of our recipes call for unsalted butter. We recommend using a European-style unsalted butter, if you can. Butter itself has a taste, so the better the quality of the butter, the better the cupcakes will be!

● **Choice of Vanilla Extract** Vanilla extract is a universal baking ingredient. It's worth splurging on a pure vanilla extract—rather than the "imitation" vanilla flavor you sometimes see at the supermarket. We absolutely love baking with Nielsen-Massey Madagascar Bourbon vanilla extract and highly recommend it.

● **Chocolate and Cocoa Powder** We love using Callebaut brand chocolate chips and Valrhona cocoa. If you can't find these brands, try to use the highest-quality chocolate and cocoa possible—it makes a huge difference!

● **Flour** Most of our recipes call for all-purpose flour. If you want to make any of the recipes gluten-free, however, you can use a gluten-free all-purpose flour blend instead. We like Bob's Red Mill brand.

- **Stand Mixer vs. Handheld Mixer** We can't live without our stand mixers, but if you don't have one at home, you can certainly bake all of these recipes using a simple handheld electric mixer/beater instead.

- **Ingredient Measurements** For each recipe, we have provided an approximate number of cupcakes or amount of other items that the recipe yields. The actual amount will depend on the size of your pans. We tend to err on the side of having too many cupcakes rather than too few, so don't worry if you have some extra batter or frosting—you can always make more!

The frosting on our cupcakes has a certain "style" to it—a perfect little cloud that reaches a pretty peak in the center. It's just the right amount of frosting—not too much, not too little—and it looks neat and sweet. Everyone is always asking us how to do it. So here, without further ado, is our secret!

Transfer your frosting into a disposable plastic piping bag fitted with a large round metal tip. Be sure to whip up your frosting so it is light and airy. You don't need to twist the top of your bag—you can just hold it closed with one hand and use your other hand to hold the bag near the bottom and squeeze.

Start in the center of the cupcake, applying pressure to the bottom of the bag, and guide the tip around the cupcake in a circular motion, then end in the center with a burst of pressure. Try to move quickly and confidently. If you go too slowly, the frosting may come out uneven. Enjoy!

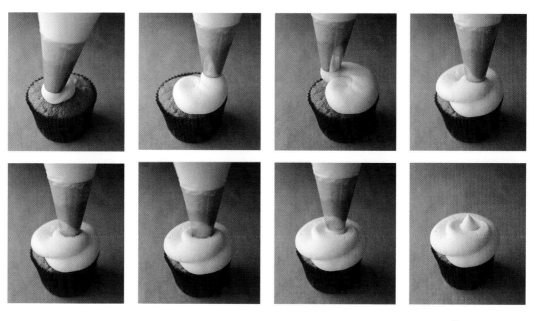

Part 1

LIFE CELEBRATIONS

From birthdays and baby showers to weddings and anniversaries, there are so many wonderful milestones in life—and reasons to throw a sweet party!

CHAPTER 1

Birthdays

Katherine's Safari Birthday

When we were little girls, there were few things more exciting than planning our birthday parties. The preparations started a month or so in advance: Mommy would ask us for our ideas—what was the theme we were thinking of, and who would we invite? There were always tons of people on the guest list, from our cousins—Mary, Elizabeth, and Annie—and neighbors to all the girls in our Sir Isaac Brock Elementary School class.

Our parties were always "Girls Only" because Mommy never let us invite boys. She was very old-fashioned that way! The only boy who ever came to our parties was our cousin Stephen, and he always felt a little out of place, surrounded by all these girls. But just because our birthdays were "Girls Only," that didn't mean they were girly-girly. In fact, for my eighth birthday, I wanted to do something wild . . . literally. The summer before, Sophie and I brought home a board game called Fireball Island. It had a tiki idol and a three-dimensional volcano, and sometimes fireball marbles would rain down as you made your way around the board. I became obsessed with this game. This year, there would be no Barbie or My Little Pony–themed bash. I wanted a one-of-a-kind tropical adventure birthday party. I wanted to turn our basement into a jungle!

When we were little girls, there were few things more exciting than planning our birthday parties.

I told everyone my idea. They looked at me like I was nuts: "Really? Nothing pink and pretty?" It was so *not* me! But I didn't care. I wanted jungle vines, ferocious animals, and a "lagoon" filled with murky water. I literally wanted to transform our basement into a full-on jungle habitat.

So Mommy took a kiddie pool and tinted the water with brown and black paint so it looked swamplike. We put up fake palm trees and tons of dark green streamers. As everyone made their way down the stairs, they were greeted by animal sounds: lions roaring, birds chirping, elephants trumpeting (we put a rain forest soundtrack on repeat on my boom box). All of us wore these cool safari party hats. We put colored plastic over the light fixtures so the lighting was very dim and had a purplish night-glow to it. It felt like we were on an expedition in the wild. All my guests were kind of spooked at first, but then they realized how cool it was.

We sat in a circle on the floor around a fake fire made of sticks and colored red, orange, and yellow tissue paper, snacking on skewered hot dogs, green veggies, and slices of tropical fruits like pineapple, mango, and papaya. For dessert, Babee, Mommy, and Sophie baked me a cake and decorated it with green buttercream grass, a blue buttercream river, Oreo soil, and a graham cracker crumb beach. They even stacked cupcakes in the center to create a "volcano" dripping with red buttercream lava. Instead of traditional birthday candles, they used long skinny candles that looked like torches.

When it was all over, no one wanted the party to end—especially me! I immediately began dreaming up what I might do the next year for my ninth birthday.

I couldn't wait to think of something even wilder!

—*Katherine*

Recipe for Success

Get Personal

Racking your brain for the perfect party theme? Think about what matters most to the guest of honor. Fill the room with personal details and unique touches so the event is all the more memorable and special. Here are some examples.

- **Use their passions as inspiration for the party theme.** Are they obsessed with a certain movie, sports team, or singer? Let their preferences guide your planning—from the décor to the food to the dress code to the music.

- **Personalize the decorations!** Order monogrammed napkins, plates, or balloons in their favorite colors.

- **Incorporate their favorite foods in the party menu wherever possible**—even in unexpected ways. For example, if they love pancakes and you aren't having a breakfast party, serve maple-flavored cupcakes!

- **Play their all-time favorite songs over the years as the party soundtrack . . .** even the most cheesy ones! It's a sure-fire way to get people dancing when they hear a song that they haven't heard in ages.

- **Get sentimental!** Put together a slide show of their life, showing photos of the guest of honor with family and friends throughout the years—silly and funny and emotional and heartfelt moments alike—and set it to music. As the photos flash on the screen, it will really hit home how special family and friends are in a person's life. Everyone is guaranteed to get teary-eyed!

Banana Chocolate Chip Monkey Cupcakes

Makes 24 cupcakes

FOR THE CUPCAKES

1¼ cups sifted all-purpose flour

1½ teaspoons baking powder

¼ teaspoon salt

¼ teaspoon ground cinnamon

¼ teaspoon ground nutmeg

8 tablespoons unsalted butter

1 cup sugar

2 large eggs

1 tablespoon honey

¼ cup water

1 cup semisweet chocolate chips

¾ cup mashed bananas

FOR THE CHOCOLATE GANACHE FROSTING

1 cup heavy cream

2 cups semisweet chocolate chips

FOR THE DECORATION

¼ pound fondant in each of your favorite colors
(for this recipe, we use yellow, white, black,
red, and brown)

piping gel

For the cupcakes:

1 Preheat the oven to 350°F. Line two cupcake pans with twelve paper baking cups each.

2 Sift together the flour, baking powder, salt, cinnamon, and nutmeg in a bowl, and set aside.

3 In the bowl of a stand mixer or in a bowl with a handheld electric mixer, cream together the butter and sugar until light and fluffy, approximately 4 to 6 minutes.

4 Add each egg slowly, one at a time, mixing after each addition.

5 Add the honey and mix slowly until just combined.

6 Add one third of the flour mixture to the butter mixture, followed by one third of the water. Mix slowly. Then add another third of the flour mixture, followed by another third of the water. Mix slowly again. Finally, add the last third of the flour mixture and the last third of the water. Mix until all the ingredients are incorporated.

7 Scrape down the bowl, and add the chocolate chips and mashed bananas. Mix slowly until well incorporated.

8 Using a standard-size ice cream scoop, fill each baking cup so that it is two-thirds full. Bake for 18 to 20 minutes or until a toothpick inserted comes out clean.

9 Let cool and set aside for frosting and decorating.

For the frosting:

1 Combine the heavy cream and chocolate chips in a medium heatproof bowl. Fill a medium saucepan with an inch or two of water and place over medium-low heat. Place the bowl over the saucepan and let the mixture melt, 15 to 20 minutes, stirring until it is shiny and smooth.

2 Remove the bowl of Chocolate Ganache from the saucepan; let it cool slightly, for 2 to 3 minutes. Working with one cupcake at a time, carefully dip each cupcake top in the warm ganache, twisting your wrist as needed to make sure the cupcake top gets completely coated.

To make the fondant monkey faces:

1 Roll out a piece of brown fondant, and using cookie cutters, cut out three circles: one with a diameter of approximately 3 inches and two with diameters of approximately 1½ inches.

2 Roll out a piece of yellow fondant, and using cookie cutters, cut out three circles: one with a diameter of approximately 1½ inches and two with diameters of approximately ¾ inches.

3 Roll out a piece of red fondant, and using a cookie cutter, cut out one circle with a diameter of approximately ¾ inches.

4 Roll out two small round balls of white fondant, about the size of a pea.

5 Roll out two very small round balls of black fondant, about the size of half a pea.

6 To assemble the monkey face on each cupcake: Place the 3-inch circle on the surface of the ganache-covered cupcake. Next, using piping gel (or water), place the three yellow circles on the monkey face so that the larger circle is at the bottom of the cupcake and the two smaller yellow circles are equally spaced above the large yellow circle. Also using piping gel to attach, place the white fondant balls on top of each of the smaller yellow circles to form the monkey's eyes. Then, attach the monkey's black pupils to the white balls by using piping gel. Attach the red circle to the large yellow circle at the bottom of the monkey's face to form the mouth. Finally, if celebrating a birthday, place a birthday candle in the red circle so the monkey has a birthday candle in its mouth!

top five rules for working with fondant

As bakers, we've developed a love-hate relationship with fondant. We love this sticky sugar dough for its versatility and the smooth, sleek look it gives cupcakes. But it can be challenging to work with. Here are some important tips to keep in mind when making the fondant decorations in this book.

1. **You can color fondant any hue you choose.** Don't worry if you can't find every shade of precolored fondant at your local cake or craft store. You need only four colors of fondant—white, red, yellow, and blue—to make every color under the rainbow. Simply knead different colors of fondant together with your hands until you achieve your desired shade. If you can find only white fondant, you can always tint it with gel food colors. Check out the photo for help with mixing colors.

2. **Keep your fondant soft.** Fondant dries out often, which makes it virtually impossible to roll or shape, and leads to cracking. The best way to keep your fondant soft is to keep it sealed in a plastic sandwich bag when it's not in use. If your fondant gets dry, pop it in the microwave for 10 to 20 seconds at a time, until it reaches a soft and pliable consistency, before you start to manipulate it.

3. **You can hide anything.** If your fondant does crack after you've already shaped it or applied it to your cupcakes, don't freak out—you can fix it! Try running your finger over the crack to smooth it out; the heat of your finger will usually do the trick. You can also add a little water to your finger and run it over the surface of the crack to moisten it. If all else fails, cover the problem area with another embellishment—a flower in a different color, a flourish, or an edible candy pearl. Nobody will ever know what lies underneath!

4. **Stick fondant together.** Invest in some piping gel to attach pieces of fondant together. Piping gel is available at all craft or cake stores and acts as edible glue. It's also transparent, so if you mess something up, you'll never be able to tell.

5. **Keep all your cookie cutters and tools clean.** We use an assortment of mini cookie cutters, scalpels, pizza wheels, and so on to cut shapes out of fondant, and it's easy for small bits of fondant to stick to the edges of these tools and build up over time. The best way to ensure that you get clean edges on all your shapes is to keep your tools—especially cookie cutters and scalpels—clean. We recommend soaking them in hot water and drying them with a paper towel after each use. ✪

Katherine and I had a great collection of dolls growing up, but one in particular was special to me. One day our dad brought us each home a surprise in a box, and we squealed with excitement as he handed them to us. She was the first dancing doll I had that could actually move on her own. She had long blond hair pulled into a bun, a delicate silver tiara, a shiny pink leotard, and a pink tutu. She had mechanical joints in her arms and legs so she could really "dance." One of her pointe shoes had a hole in the tip so it could be attached to her purple dance platform. The platform had a shiny silver floor surface and several steps, and controls on the bottom so I could direct her movements. With the press of a button she would be doing beautiful pirouettes to the music from *Swan Lake*.

I was mesmerized by my doll and played with her for hours on end. Inspired, Katherine and I started taking ballet classes and I slowly learned to imitate my doll's movements, moving my feet from first position to second to third to fourth and finally fifth. I tried to balance myself as I learned to grand plié and pirouette. I even wanted to dress like my ballerina doll and became obsessed with tulle and tiaras. I had a pink tulle skirt and a small crystal tiara that I begged to wear to school every day—though Mommy would never let me. How would I look parading into second grade in a tiara? She shook her head: "No way, Sophie."

To make it up to me, Mommy surprised me with a beautiful ballerina-themed seventh-birthday party. She decorated the house with swathes of pink and purple tulle, twinkling lights, and lots of pink and purple satin ribbon bows. We drank from pink crystal goblets, and she served sandwiches on beautiful crystal pink dishes and antique pink cake stands. Katherine and I wore color-coordinated pink and purple tank tops and tutus, and I got to wear my tiara all day. I even had a little ballerina dancer on top of my pink and purple cake. I loved every part of it!

During the party, Katherine and I choreographed our own ballet dance routine and practiced and practiced. We recruited our cousins to take part in the "recital," too. After much rehearsing we cleared the living room, rounded up all the adults, and sat them down for the big performance. Babee, Papou, our parents, and all our other family members were there. We hit the music on the tape recorder, and the bedsheet curtains we jerry-rigged flew up! Even though we were probably really bad dancers, and all our timing was off, everyone applauded loudly as we took our bows. It was a magical birthday, from start to finish.

—*Sophie*

mixing and matching with recipes

Are you a fan of chocolate, but not peanut butter? Or vanilla, but not lemon? If you find a recipe in this book that intrigues you, it's okay to mix and match the batter from one recipe with the frosting from another. All of the batter and frosting recipes in this book can be swapped according to your taste buds! And you can completely change the look of the finished product with some simple substitutions. Check out what the giant cupcake (see page 18) looks like when dressed up with different frostings and decorations. ✖

Yellow buttercream frosting and rainbow sprinkles.

Vanilla cream cheese frosting and shredded coconut.

Strawberry buttercream frosting and fresh strawberries.

Vanilla buttercream frosting and pink fondant flowers.

Raspberry Buttercream "Tutu" Cupcakes

Makes 24 cupcakes

2½ cups sifted all-purpose flour

2½ teaspoons baking powder

¼ teaspoon salt

8 tablespoons unsalted butter

1¾ cups sugar

2 large eggs

2¼ teaspoons pure vanilla extract

1¼ cups whole milk

1 cup fresh raspberries

16 tablespoons unsalted butter

4 cups sifted confectioners' sugar

1 teaspoon whole milk

1 teaspoon pure vanilla extract

¼ teaspoon salt

½ cup fresh raspberries, diced

24 whole fresh raspberries,
   for garnish

For the cupcakes:

1 Preheat the oven to 350°F. Line two cupcake pans with twelve paper baking cups each.

2 Sift together the flour, baking powder, and salt in a bowl, and set aside.

3 Place the butter in the bowl of a stand mixer or in a bowl with a handheld electric mixer. Add the sugar; beat on medium speed until well incorporated, approximately 3 to 5 minutes.

4 Add the eggs one at a time, mixing slowly after each addition.

5 Combine the vanilla extract and milk and in a large liquid measuring cup.

6 Add one third of the flour mixture to the butter mixture, then gradually add one third of the milk mixture, beating slowly until well incorporated. Add another third of the flour mixture, followed by another third of the milk mixture. Stop to scrape down the bowl as needed. Add the remaining flour mixture, followed by the remaining milk mixture, and beat just until combined.

7 Using a spatula, gently fold in the raspberries.

8 Scoop batter into the baking cups so that each is two-thirds full, and bake for 16 to 18 minutes or until a toothpick inserted into the center of a cupcake comes out clean. Transfer the pans to a wire rack to cool completely.

For the frosting:

1 Place the butter in the bowl of a stand mixer or in a bowl with a handheld electric mixer. Add the confectioners' sugar; beat on medium speed until well incorporated. Add the milk, vanilla extract, and salt. Finally, add the diced raspberries and beat until well incorporated and the frosting is light and fluffy, approximately 3 to 4 minutes.

2 Frost your cupcakes using Georgetown Cupcake's signature swirl technique (see page xxv), and top each one with a fresh raspberry.

Sophie turned thirty the summer we were planning on opening Georgetown Cupcake. At the time we were saving all of our money to go toward the business, so I didn't have a big budget to throw her a lavish birthday party or take her and a group of friends out to a fancy dinner. Every nickel we had went into our store. At the same time, turning thirty is a major milestone, so I wanted to do something special for Sophie. I decided to turn her dining room table into a colorful Decorate-Your-Own Cupcake Bar! She was always getting on my case and giving me a guilt trip about not working hard enough, so my idea was perfect. We could party *and* experiment with new cupcake decorating ideas at the same time!

> *We could party and experiment with new cupcake decorating ideas at the same time!*

All it took was a white linen tablecloth, some white porcelain bowls and spoons, and a whole lot of colorful cupcake toppings and frostings. I quickly baked up two dozen of our chocolate cupcakes and lined them up on the table—our canvases were ready! And before she got home, I baked a giant cupcake, decorated it just for her, and put a candle on it.

When she walked through the door, Steve and I shouted, "Happy birthday!" and I handed Sophie the big cupcake. She smiled as she took in the table, with all the colorful and glittery sugar, sprinkles, and toppings. We spent the next three hours decorating and talking about our menu and what the cupcakes would look like. It was a low-key but fun birthday, full of conversation and laughter. Plus it got our creative juices flowing! That was the night Sophie came up with our Chocolate Hazelnut cupcake, which is still her favorite to this day!

—*Katherine*

making a decorate-your-own "happy birthday" cupcake bar

Setting up a Decorate-Your-Own Cupcake Bar is fun and easy! First, cover your table with a solid-colored tablecloth. We like using a plain or textured white tablecloth, as it will let the color palette of your toppings bar really shine. Then arrange a series of shallow dishes in a line down the length of the table. Fill the dishes with your favorite cupcake toppings, such as chocolate and rainbow-colored sprinkles, candy pieces like toffee, crushed cookies, chopped nuts, chocolate chips, and fondant decorations like flowers, hearts, and other fun shapes and designs. Arrange bowls of beautifully hued frostings with spatulas and piping bags. Also, include several squeeze bottles of hot fudge and caramel sauce. Place unfrosted cupcakes on display on multileveled tiers, and then invite your guests to get creative and decorate their most perfect cupcake! To add even more excitement, award prizes for the most attractive or unusual designs, or have each cupcake capture something special about the birthday boy or girl.

TIP: Cupcake bars are not just an option for casual and fun birthdays. They are definitely appropriate for more upscale celebrations as well. If you want to make your cupcake bar look more "chic" for a fancier event, try putting together a monochromatic cupcake bar in the color scheme of the event. Choose toppings and candies of different types in one color. This totally changes the look and feel of the cupcake bar and gives it a more sophisticated and refined appearance. It's the same idea, but by keeping all the toppings in one color, you can transform your cupcake bar from whimsical to sleek! ✴

Giant Chocolate Hazelnut Cupcake

This is Sophie's all-time favorite cupcake flavor, and this recipe makes a fun birthday cake! If you don't like hazelnuts, you can substitute your favorite cupcake topping—rainbow-colored sprinkles, shredded coconut, or your favorite candy (see page 13 for mixing and matching with different looks). For this recipe, you'll need a giant two-sided cupcake pan, measuring roughly $6 \times 8 \times 4$ inches. You can find one in the baking aisle of your local craft or specialty cooking store.

Serves 8

FOR THE GIANT CUPCAKE

1¼ cups sifted all-purpose flour

½ teaspoon baking soda

¼ teaspoon salt

8 tablespoons unsalted butter

1¼ cups sugar

2 large eggs

1¼ teaspoons pure vanilla extract

1 cup whole milk

½ cup sifted cocoa powder

FOR THE CHOCOLATE GANACHE AND HAZELNUT CRUNCH TOPPING

½ cup heavy cream

1 cup semisweet chocolate chips

4 cups crushed hazelnut pieces

For the giant cupcake:

1 Preheat the oven to 350°F. Grease your giant cupcake pan with butter, and set aside.

2 Sift together the flour, baking soda, and salt in a bowl, and set aside.

3 Place the butter in the bowl of a stand mixer or in a bowl with a handheld electric mixer. Beat on medium speed until fluffy. Stop to add the sugar; then beat on medium speed until well incorporated, approximately 3 to 5 minutes. Add the eggs one at a time, mixing slowly after each addition.

4 Combine the vanilla extract and milk in a large liquid measuring cup.

5 Add one third of the flour mixture to the butter mixture, then gradually add one third of the milk mixture, beating slowly until well incorporated. Add another third of the flour mixture, followed by another third of the milk mixture. Stop to scrape down the bowl as needed. Add the remaining flour mixture, followed by the remaining milk mixture, and mix slowly until just combined.

6 Add the cocoa powder, mixing on low speed until just incorporated.

7 Pour the chocolate batter into both sides of the giant cupcake pan. Bake for 24 to 26 minutes (start checking at 24 minutes) or until a toothpick inserted into the center of the cupcake comes out clean. Transfer the pan to a wire rack to cool completely.

For the topping:

1 Combine the heavy cream and chocolate chips in a medium heatproof bowl. Fill a medium saucepan with an inch or two of water and place over medium-low heat. Place the bowl over the saucepan and let the mixture melt, stirring continuously until it is shiny and smooth.

2 Remove the bowl of Chocolate Ganache from the saucepan; let it cool slightly for 2 to 3 minutes. Take the top half of the giant cupcake and dip it into the Chocolate Ganache, then turn it right side up and place it on the wax paper. Allow the ganache to set for 5 minutes before proceeding.

3 Cover the top half of the cupcake with crushed hazelnut pieces. Be sure to cover the entire top surface of the cupcake, and save any excess hazelnuts. Pour 1 tablespoon of the remaining ganache on the bottom half of the cupcake (to act as glue), then cover with the top of the cupcake. Insert candles (if this is a birthday cupcake), and enjoy!

CHAPTER ⊚ 2

··

Bridal Showers

As Katherine's big sister and matron of honor, I was in charge of planning her bridal shower—so it had to be amazing. More than a hundred female family members and friends came to shower Katherine with love. In Greek families, bridal showers are basically mini weddings—just for women!

The theme of the shower was "An Afternoon Garden Cupcake Tea Party." Mommy and I worked very hard on this event and planned everything down to the smallest detail. There was a lot of tense last-minute scrambling to get everything done, but the end result was so breathtaking, it rendered my sis totally speechless (a rarity for her!). She couldn't believe all the special touches—and special cupcakes—I incorporated into her party.

For the venue, I chose a historic home with beautiful gardens, where the guests could roam on the terrace and green lawn, and mingle among the flowers and fountains. Of course, the color scheme for the shower was *pink*—just like our Georgetown Cupcake packaging. I selected Peony Pink taffeta linens for the tables and had beautiful glass urns brimming with pink garden roses and hydrangea. The classic gold Chiavari chairs and gold chargers on the tables provided a perfect accent color.

It goes without saying that cupcakes were *everywhere* at Katherine's bridal shower, but I didn't just serve them for dessert. I used them in a variety of creative ways. Instead of numbering the tables, we named each table after one of our Georgetown Cupcake flavors. So instead of seating guests at Table 1, Table 2, Table 3, and so on, we seated them at Red Velvet, Lava Fudge, Salted Caramel, Peanut Butter Fudge, Vanilla Squared, Chocolate Coconut, Maple, Chocolate and Vanilla, Lemon Blossom, Lemon Berry, and Mocha.

Instead of paper place cards, I placed each of the guests' names on a mini cupcake of the corresponding table flavor. So each guest had to find her place card and then see which flavor she had (taking a bite was the easiest and most delicious way!). It was like a game, and it got everyone talking and mingling and discussing flavors.

To go with the tea party theme, I created a special cupcake flavor just for Katherine's bridal shower: a Lavender Earl Grey Teacake cupcake. I infused Katherine's favorite blend of lavender and Earl Grey teas in the cupcake batter as well as the buttercream icing. Then I made a huge cupcake sculpture centerpiece—a giant teapot made out of cupcakes that pumped real tea.

Finally, there was my baking-inspired gift to my little sister. Some people collect stamps, some people collect cars . . . we collect mixers! I know how crazy Katherine is about our mixer collection, so I wanted to get her a mixer that nobody else in the world had—something one-of-a-kind, made just for her. So I bought her a custom hot pink mixer covered in thousands of pink Swarovski crystals! When she opened her blinged-out mixer, she absolutely *freaked*! She loved it, and I was so happy. To this day, it stands on display at our Georgetown Cupcake SoHo store, one of Katherine's most treasured possessions.

As a parting gift, shower guests took home four mini cupcakes in Katherine's favorite flavors (Peanut Butter Fudge, Salted Caramel, Lava Fudge, and Vanilla Squared), a tiny package of her special tea blend, and a recipe card for Katherine's Lavender Earl Grey Teacake cupcakes. The four hours of the shower flew by. We laughed, we cried . . . and we ate *tons* of cupcakes!

—*Sophie*

Katherine's Bridal Shower Lavender Earl Grey Teacake Cupcakes

We love these cupcakes infused with just the right amount of lavender. If you like, for an extra touch, you can place a fondant flower on top of each cupcake and serve each one in a china teacup!

Makes 18 cupcakes

FOR THE CUPCAKES

2½ cups sifted all-purpose flour

2½ teaspoons baking powder

¼ teaspoon salt

8 tablespoons unsalted butter

1¾ cups granulated sugar

2 large eggs

2¼ teaspoons pure vanilla extract

1¼ cups whole milk

½ cup extra-strong lavender Earl Grey tea, cooled

2 teaspoons lavender sugar (optional)

FOR THE LAVENDER BUTTERCREAM FROSTING

16 tablespoons unsalted butter

4 cups sifted confectioners' sugar

1 teaspoon whole milk

1 teaspoon pure vanilla extract

⅛ teaspoon salt

¼ cup extra-strong lavender Earl Grey tea, cooled

¼ cup lavender sugar, plus extra for decoration (optional)

¼ teaspoon purple food color

For the cupcakes:

1 Preheat the oven to 350°F. Line a cupcake pan with twelve paper baking cups and a second pan with six baking cups.

2 Sift together the flour, baking powder, and salt in a bowl, and set aside.

3 Place the butter in the bowl of a stand mixer or in a bowl with a handheld electric mixer. Add the granulated sugar; beat on medium speed until well incorporated, approximately 3 to 5 minutes.

4 Add the eggs one at a time, mixing slowly after each addition.

5 Combine the vanilla extract and milk in a large liquid measuring cup.

6 Add one third of the flour mixture to the butter mixture, then gradually add one third of the milk mixture, beating slowly until well incorporated. Add another third of the flour mixture, followed by another third of the milk mixture. Stop to scrape down the bowl as needed. Add the remaining flour mixture, followed by the remaining milk mixture, and beat just until combined.

7 Mix in the tea and lavender sugar until fully incorporated.

8 Scoop batter into the baking cups so that each is two-thirds full, and bake for

18 minutes or until a toothpick inserted into the center of a cupcake comes out clean. Transfer the pans to a wire rack to cool completely.

For the frosting:

Place the butter in the bowl of a stand mixer or in a bowl with a handheld electric mixer. Add the confectioners' sugar; beat on medium speed until well incorporated. Add the milk, vanilla extract, salt, tea, lavender sugar, and purple food color, and beat on high speed until light and airy. Frost the cupcakes using a signature swirl (see page xxv), and sprinkle lavender sugar on top.

The Right Mix

Developing a seating plan for your special event can be a stressful task, but it doesn't have to be! I made the mistake of leaving Mommy in charge of our seating plan for Katherine's bridal shower, and you can find out what trouble ensued on page 251. A good seating plan provides an opportunity for family members to reunite, for friends and colleagues to make new acquaintances, and for guests of honor to be celebrated. For bridal showers and wedding parties, one good rule of thumb is to seat the parents and siblings of the bride and groom with each other at the same table, often adjacent to the special couple. This can symbolize the union of two families. Another common approach is to seat close friends from different phases of life with each other at the same table. Invariably, the guests at the table will begin to share stories about the guest(s) of honor at various stages in their lives. As a result, everyone at the table leaves with a full appreciation of how special their friend and colleague is. If you can, have your head table located in the center of the room, so that nobody is located in the back and there is a cozy and intimate feeling among all tables.

—*Sophie*

Katherine's bridal shower.

Katherine's Bridal Shower Pink "Mocktails"

We served these mocktails in unique stemless champagne flutes with cute pink and white striped straws—the perfect touch! If you want to make them alcoholic, you can replace the sparkling water and white grape juice with champagne.

Makes 24 champagne flutes/glasses

6 cups sparkling water
6 cups sparkling white grape juice
1 cup cranberry juice
4 pints fresh raspberries

❶ In a large punch bowl, using a large spoon, mix together the sparkling water, grape juice, and cranberry juice. Refrigerate for at least 1 hour.

❷ Pour into each champagne flute, and drop one or two fresh raspberries into each flute. Serve with pink and white striped drinking straws, and with champagne flutes all lined up on a silver platter.

sisters' secret
using cupcake flavors instead of table numbers

At most large seated events, you find your seat by finding out your table number and then looking for that number at the center of one of the tables. To "sweeten" things up for your guests, instead of using table numbers, why not label each table with a cupcake flavor, as we did for Katherine's bridal shower? One table could be called Red Velvet, another Chocolate Coconut, another Salted Caramel, and so on. Place each guest's name on a small card attached to a toothpick, and place the card atop a mini cupcake in the flavor of the table where they'll be sitting. Guests pick up the mini cupcake with their name on it, then find the table that corresponds to its flavor. It's a fun way to get guests talking and break the ice before a big event. ✱

CHAPTER 3

Weddings

Katherine's Wedding

One of the best perks of planning a wedding is the ability to indulge your sweet tooth! My sweetest personal celebration, without a doubt, was my wedding day, Saturday, September 17, 2011, in Montecito, California. After eight years of dating Ben, I was *finally* getting married. Ever since I was a little girl, I dreamed of what my wedding would be like. The flowers, the dress, the music, the food, the works—it was like a full-on fairy tale. And now it was becoming a reality!

We had only ten months to plan the wedding, and they flew by. It was a whirl-wind of activity, designing a wedding across the country in California while also running the bakery back in Washington, DC. Luckily, I had a lot of help from a fantastic wedding planner, Sharon Sacks, and a great sister! Once Ben and I toured

San Ysidro Ranch in the hills of Santa Barbara, we knew it was the place we wanted to get married. It had all the natural beauty you could imagine, and an amazing view of the ocean. There was something magical about this place, but it was very peaceful at the same time. There were lemon trees growing all over the property, and the aroma of fresh lemons permeated the air.

But this fairy tale did not come about without some major bumps in the road. What good is a happy ending if there are no mishaps and adventures along the way? The first challenge was getting a huge wedding cupcake tower baked, decorated, and transported to the site. I already knew that Sophie wanted to make my wedding cupcake tower for me. I was worried because it was such a large project for her to undertake on her own, and I knew that I was going to be preoccupied the week before the wedding and unable to help her. She also wanted to keep the flavor, style, and size of the cupcakes a secret from me. She told me I wouldn't be disappointed. It's a good thing I trust her so much! So I left the cupcake tower in Sophie's capable hands.

I woke up on the day of my wedding *so* excited! I jumped out of bed, ordered breakfast, and walked around the ranch in my pj's! I watched as the chuppah was being constructed and decorated with flowers, and dozens of people rushed around setting up the tent. It was hard to believe this was all for Ben and me!

The ceremony was beautiful, and the reception was a blast. When I walked into the room to dance with my husband to our first song, the wedding cupcake tower Sophie had created was front and center. My jaw dropped in amazement. The sheer size of it blew me away. It was made from over 5,000 champagne-flavored cupcakes and was over nine feet tall! I couldn't believe the work Sophie had done to make my dream wedding cake. I could not have imagined something more beautiful than what she made. It was everything I could have dreamed of. The cupcakes were ivory and white and matched everything in the room perfectly. It was spectacular and elegant all at the same time. The flavor was just as elegant, a champagne buttercream cupcake. She even used my favorite champagne, Moët & Chandon!

—*Katherine*

creating the perfect wedding cupcake tower

You don't have to create a cupcake tower that's nine feet tall to achieve a "wow" factor at your wedding. You can make a beautiful tower centerpiece with as few as a hundred cupcakes. The best way to display a tower is on a single small round or square table, draped with a tablecloth. There are many different manufacturers of cupcake towers, so you can use a premade structure, or you can easily build one yourself for a fraction of the cost. These towers are also great for Sweet Sixteen parties, engagement parties, or any other formal occasion. Simply cut square pieces of foam of the same height, but each one 6 inches smaller on each side. Depending on how many cupcakes you would like to display, here are some benchmark measurements for cupcake towers of various sizes:

Size of Foam Squares in Inches

Number of Cupcakes to Be Served	6x6	12x12	18x18	24x24	30x30	36x36	42x42	48x48	54x54	60x60
100	✴	✴	✴	✴						
150	✴	✴	✴	✴	✴					
200	✴	✴	✴	✴	✴	✴				
250	✴	✴	✴	✴	✴	✴	✴			
300	✴	✴	✴	✴	✴	✴	✴	✴		
400	✴	✴	✴	✴	✴	✴	✴	✴	✴	
500	✴	✴	✴	✴	✴	✴	✴	✴	✴	✴

Once you have cut your pieces of foam, wrap them in a fabric of your choice, pinning the fabric to the foam with flat-top pins. Try to coordinate the fabric color with the wedding color scheme. We find that solid-colored fabrics look best. Then wrap a single strand of complementary-colored ribbon around each tower foam block. Tie the ribbon so that the bow is in the corner, providing a pretty accent. Stack the fabric-covered foam blocks on top of each other, and place cupcakes around each level. Use fresh flowers (coordinating with the wedding flowers) to accent the tower on each level. Remember—one of the best parts of making a cupcake tower for your wedding is the ability to mix and match your favorite cupcake flavors—you don't have to commit to just one! ✴

Recipe for Success

Make Your Guests Feel Welcome

$\mathcal{I}$f you are having a destination wedding with a lot of guests coming in from out of town, a thoughtful way to welcome them is to leave a box of a half-dozen cupcakes in their hotel rooms with a welcome note and itinerary attached. For my wedding, a lot of our guests were traveling from a long distance, and some were even coming from abroad. I wanted to set the stage for the rest of the festivities that weekend. So when guests arrived in their hotel rooms, there was a pink Georgetown Cupcake box gift-wrapped and waiting on their beds. Inside it were cupcakes in Ben's and my favorite flavors: Peanut Butter Fudge, Salted Caramel, Chocolate Coconut, Vanilla Buttercream, Red Velvet, and Lemon Blossom. I customized the fondant with our "KB" emblem (for Katherine and Ben), but you can also use your wedding locale as your inspiration. For example, if you are having a beach-themed wedding, go for an assortment of flavors like Coconut, Key Lime, and Mango, and have them decorated with fondant flip-flops. If you are having a winter wedding, include flavors like Gingerbread and Chocolate Peppermint, and have them decorated with fondant snowflakes.

Send Your Guests Off on a Sweet Note

*Y*ou can also use cupcakes to give your guests a sweet send-off. For my wedding, I wanted each guest to leave with a special individual cupcake box after a long night of dancing. The ranch's lemon trees were amazing: the Meyer lemons were huge and ripe. So we had our staff hand-pick, zest, and squeeze fresh lemons into the batter to make Lemon Blossom cupcakes. Each one was again topped with a "KB" emblem. We packed them individually into our signature pink Georgetown Cupcake boxes with a note that read "Sweet Dreams." It was the perfect end to a perfect night!

For a personal touch, choose your favorite flavor of cupcake and decorate it with a fondant piece in the shape of your new monogram or your wedding date, and then individually box and gift-wrap one for each guest with a thank-you note. Or, if your budget allows, create a custom assortment of mini cupcakes of different flavors, gift-wrapped for each guest to enjoy.

—*Katherine*

Champagne Cupcakes with Champagne Buttercream and Fondant Monograms and Roses

Makes 18 cupcakes

FOR THE CUPCAKES

2½ cups sifted all-purpose flour

½ teaspoon baking powder

¼ teaspoon salt

8 tablespoons unsalted butter

1¾ cups sugar

2 large eggs

2¼ teaspoons pure vanilla extract

1¼ cups whole milk

½ cup champagne

FOR THE CHAMPAGNE
BUTTERCREAM FROSTING

16 tablespoons unsalted butter

4 cups sifted confectioners' sugar

1 teaspoon whole milk

1 teaspoon pure vanilla extract

⅛ teaspoon salt

¼ cup champagne

¼ cup white sanding sugar (optional), for
   dusting

FOR THE DECORATION

¼ pound fondant in your favorite color

fondant roller

rubber letter stamps

circle or flower cookie cutter

pink and green food color

teardrop- and leaf-shaped cookie cutters or
   scalpel

For the cupcakes:

1 Preheat the oven to 350°F. Line a cupcake pan with twelve paper baking cups and a second pan with six baking cups.

2 Sift together the flour, baking powder, and salt in a bowl, and set aside.

3 Place the butter in the bowl of a stand mixer or in a bowl with a handheld electric mixer. Add the sugar; beat on medium speed until well incorporated.

4 Add the eggs one at a time, mixing slowly after each addition.

5 Combine the vanilla extract and milk in a large liquid measuring cup.

6 Add one third of the flour mixture to the butter mixture, then gradually add one third of the milk mixture, beating slowly until well incorporated. Add another third of the flour mixture, followed by another third of the milk mixture. Stop to scrape down the bowl as needed. Add the remaining flour mixture, followed by the remaining milk mixture, and beat just until combined.

7 Mix in the champagne until fully incorporated.

8 Scoop batter into the baking cups so that each is two-thirds full, and bake for 18 minutes or until a toothpick inserted into the center of a cupcake comes out clean. Transfer the pans to a wire rack to cool completely.

For the frosting:

Place the butter in the bowl of a stand mixer or in a bowl with a handheld electric mixer. Add the confectioners' sugar; beat on medium speed until well incorporated. Add the milk, vanilla extract, salt, and champagne, and beat on high speed until light and airy. Frost cupcakes using a signature swirl (see page xxv), and sprinkle sanding sugar on top so that the top is completely covered.

To make the fondant monograms:

To make the fondant monograms, roll out a piece of fondant in your desired color and press a rubber letter stamp in the fondant to make an imprint. (You can purchase rubber-stamp alphabet sets in any craft store.) Then cut out the fondant piece in a disc or flower shape and place on each cupcake.

To make the fondant roses:

To make the fondant roses, roll out a small ball of fondant the size of a walnut. Pull the top so that it is long and narrow and looks like a teardrop. Then roll out and cut out teardrop-shaped pieces of fondant. One by one, layer the fondant teardrops on top of the fondant ball, forming the petals of the rose. Push back some of the petals to create volume in your rose. Set on a surface to harden. Then paint your rose with food color to match your color theme. To make leaves for your roses, roll out fondant and cut out leaf shapes using a leaf-shaped cutter or a scalpel. Lay on top of your fondant roller or another curved surface to get a curved shape. Once dry, paint with food color to create a beautiful green color. Place a rose and 2 or 3 leaves on top of each cupcake.

Steve and I became engaged two years after we graduated from Princeton together. As I was the first one in the family to become engaged, Mommy was ecstatic. That did not mean we didn't butt heads in the planning process, however. I wanted an elegant city evening affair; Mommy wanted something more akin to *My Big Fat Greek Wedding*. Luckily, I prevailed. Since our family was much larger than Steve's family, we got married in Toronto and I did all of my planning long distance from Washington, DC.

I planned the wedding for a year after our engagement, so I had plenty of time to obsess over all the details. We ended up getting married on August 16, 2003, quite a re-

markable weekend (see page 46 for the details). We had a seated dinner for two hundred guests, and I chose a palette of dark red roses in glass cubes for the centerpieces, cream-colored silk tablecloths, and cocoa Chiavari chairs. Dessert was a little more complicated. In addition to our chocolate espresso wedding cake, we wanted to serve a separate plated dessert of fancy cupcakes out of their wrappers. I love all things chocolate-based, and Steve loves all things vanilla-based. So, to compromise, we served alternating plates of mini cakes and sorbets—so that one guest had chocolate and the person seated beside them had vanilla. This is a great way to encourage guests to share their desserts!

—*Sophie*

(see page 46 for the details)

sisters' secret
mini cupcakes for a midnight wedding buffet

After guests have been dancing the night away, they need a little fuel to keep the party going. If you are planning on a midnight buffet of bite-size snacks (e.g., mini burgers and grilled cheese), mini cupcakes are a perfect addition. Pick a ton of different flavors and either have the waitstaff serve them on cocktail trays to guests on the dance floor or arrange them on a small buffet table in the shape of a heart or spelling out your monogram, your wedding date, or another sweet message! ✱

Marble Mini Cupcakes

This recipe for marble minis is based on Babee's marble cake—a staple for dessert in our house when we were little. Since the cupcakes themselves look so beautiful with their marbled pattern, you can serve them "naked"—without frosting. I love making these marble minis because they represent both Steve's and my favorite flavors, swirled together, and remind me of our wedding desserts. These marble cupcakes are so elegant, they are perfect to serve for dessert at a formal affair.

Makes 48 mini cupcakes

2¼ cups sifted all-purpose flour

2½ teaspoons baking powder

16 tablespoons unsalted butter

1¼ cups sugar

4 large eggs

¾ cup vanilla yogurt

½ cup whole milk

2½ tablespoons sifted cocoa powder

1 Preheat the oven to 350°F and line two mini cupcake pans with twenty-four mini baking cups each.

2 Sift together the flour and baking powder in a bowl, and set aside.

3 In the bowl of a stand mixer or in a bowl with a handheld electric mixer, cream together the butter and sugar until light and fluffy, approximately 3 to 5 minutes.

4 Add the eggs slowly, one at a time, mixing after each addition.

5 Add the yogurt, mixing until fully incorporated.

6 Add one half of the flour mixture to the butter mixture in the bowl and mix slowly; add one half of the milk and mix slowly, stopping to scrape down the bowl. Add the last half of the flour mixture, followed by the remaining half of the milk.

7 Divide batter in half, and set half aside. To the half remaining in the bowl of the mixer, add cocoa powder.

8 Using a mini ice cream scoop, transfer the vanilla batter into each baking cup so that it is one-third full. Next, scoop a roughly equal amount of the chocolate batter on top of the vanilla batter in each baking cup and, using a toothpick, swirl together the chocolate and vanilla batter.

9 Bake for 12 to 14 minutes or until a toothpick inserted comes out clean. Transfer the pans to a wire rack to cool completely. To serve, place several mini cupcakes on a plate with a small scoop of chocolate or vanilla sorbet.

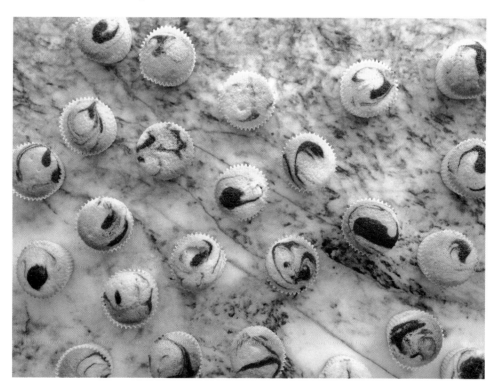

Recipe for Success

Don't Sweat the Small Stuff

Two days before my wedding, Katherine and I were at the spa in Toronto, getting our nails done for my big day. As I sat in the spa chair, I was silently going through my remaining "To Do" list before the wedding on Saturday: pick up my wedding dress and veil, pick up Katherine's bridesmaid dress, pick up Mommy's dress, check on the flowers, wrap the favors, do the seating chart and place cards . . .

The spa that day was a whirlwind of activity—every seat was full and the hair dryers were blowing at a loud roar, drowning out the conversations of all the women. Then, all of a sudden, the lights went out and everything went silent. Everyone looked around at one another, confused, but the salon manager let out a huge laugh. *We must have blown a fuse with all these hair dryers going!* So she went to the back to figure out how to turn the power on.

Several minutes passed and some women wandered out of the salon to get some fresh air, only to return with startling news—the power on the entire *block* was out! Katherine and I slowly walked out to the street and looked around—all the streetlights around us and the stoplights were out. We looked out at the sky-scrapers in the distance—all their lights were out too. I started to feel a little uneasy. I picked up my cell phone and called Steve. He sounded very anxious and quietly told me that it wasn't just our block or our city that was blacked out—it was *the entire Northeast,* from New York to Michigan and everywhere in between.

I started to panic. "When is the power coming back on?" I asked Steve. "We're getting married in two days! How are we going to have our wedding in the dark?"

Steve tried to calm me down and came and took me back to our dark hotel. All of a sudden, all of the planning I had done did not mean a thing. Nobody knew when the power was going to be restored; some reports said it would be weeks! All flights in the region were cancelled, and all businesses were shut down. While Steve called all our out-of-town guests to help them figure out alternate travel arrangements, I immediately ran to the Vera Wang boutique to try to retrieve my wedding dress and Katherine's bridesmaid dress. Sure enough, it had closed early for the day due to the blackout. I called and I called—no answer—and left what seemed like a million messages.

As I walked back to the hotel, I felt helpless. I forced myself to go to sleep and hope for the best. But when I woke up the next morning, there was still no power. I started to feel the sinking feeling in my stomach again. Suddenly, my cell phone rang and it was my wedding planner. The Vera Wang boutique was going to send somebody in to let us pick up my dress! I immediately felt re-energized. Instead of wallowing in my sadness, I decided to take action. I was going to tackle all of our problems, one by one.

First up was the rehearsal dinner. The restaurant still did not have power, so we quickly bought a ton of beautiful candles and planned a candlelight dinner. The restaurant set up grills outside and grilled all of the food. Our priest, who was to marry us, was still stranded in Washington, DC, so we asked the priest who had taught all of our Pre-Cana wedding classes if he could marry us. Of course, he said yes.

After our beautiful rehearsal dinner, I felt more at ease and ready for anything that came my way. Suddenly, I wasn't obsessing about the spacing on the place cards, or the placement of the roses in the centerpieces. While I loved planning the details, I realized that there are some things in life that are just simply out of your control. You need to go with the flow. The blackout got me to focus on what was most important: I was getting married to the love of my life. I was able to let go of the little things, not sweat the small stuff, and enjoy this important day in my life even more.

The next morning, by some miracle, the power came back on, just in time for the wedding. Steve gave the sweetest toast to me at the reception. He said, "I wish the power was still off, because when I saw you walk down that aisle . . . you could have lit up the entire city."

—Sophie

CHAPTER ⊚ 4

Anniversaries

Our First Anniversary

After a honeymoon on the island of Santorini, Greece, Steve and I packed up our belongings and moved from Washington, DC, to Cambridge, Massachusetts, where Steve was going to start graduate school. At around the same time I had started a new job in Boston, so we were both working nonstop. We'd wake up in the morning, work all day long, and then come home and work even longer.

When we got home, I had to figure out what I was going to make for dinner. As anyone knows, coming up with a creative menu, day in and day out, especially when you are exhausted, is hard. And if anyone was going to cook, it was going to be me. Steve was a little "challenged" in the kitchen. Steve is a genius, but after I caught him

49

seasoning grilled chicken with ground cinnamon, I banned him from the kitchen forever. So dinners became my task.

So you can imagine my shock when I came home on the night of our first anniversary and found that Steve had cooked a romantic homemade dinner for two. When I walked in the door, I was greeted with an amazing smell coming from the kitchen. I looked at our dining table and saw that Steve had placed fresh roses in a vase, and even set our good china and silver *correctly* on the table.

"Should I be scared?" I chuckled.

"Don't worry!" Steve assured me, pulling out my chair. "Sit down. Relax!" he said.

The appetizer was a goat cheese and fig crostini. Then came the first course—a roasted red pepper soup that he garnished with crème fraîche and a sprig of basil. Next, he brought out a whole rosemary chicken with roasted potatoes and vegetables all around it. Where was he getting all this stuff from? Did he order from a restaurant and plate it on our home china? I couldn't believe how good everything was.

But it was true—Steve had cooked all of it himself. He confessed that he had been researching recipes all week long, trying to pick the perfect menu, and studying them to make sure he didn't screw anything up. He came home from school early that day and cooked all afternoon. It was the most romantic dinner ever.

sisters' secret

a small dusting is a sweet finish to any dessert

When in a bind about how to jazz up a cake or any other completed dessert, try a simple dusting of confectioners' sugar on chocolate or dark-colored desserts, or cocoa, espresso, or cinnamon powder on lighter-colored desserts. If you really want to get fancy, try a dusting of ground-up gold leaf to add a little sparkle. "Dusting" quickly transforms a rather ordinary-looking dessert into something chic and elegant! ✸

For dessert, we opened our freezer door for something we had been looking forward to eating all year: the top of our wedding cake! Like most wedding couples, we saved the top tier to eat on our first anniversary. Our wedding cake was chocolate and espresso cake with a coffee liqueur buttercream. Steve, in all his dinner preparations, had forgotten to take it out of the freezer earlier, so it was still rock hard. We tried to be patient, and waited, waited, waited for the cake to thaw. Finally we couldn't wait any longer, so we served up our half-frozen wedding cake in glass ice cream dishes and dug in. It was delicious—just as we remembered—and the perfect way to end Steve's surprise anniversary dinner.

—*Sophie*

Recipe for Success

The Element of Surprise

When Steve caught me off guard with a surprise dinner on our first anniversary, it was meaningful not only because he spent the entire day preparing it and because it was our anniversary, but also because it was completely unexpected. The next year, I decided to return the surprise by making him breakfast in bed—delicious warm muffins. When entertaining, you can take the element of surprise even further: For dessert, try adding a surprise filling to your cupcakes, use a super-hard-to-get ingredient that the guest of honor loves, or impress your guests with a dramatic presentation by placing lit sparklers in your cupcakes or cakes. That little extra element of surprise goes a long way in making your celebration memorable. —*Sophie*

Anniversary Cupcake Dessert: Chocolate Espresso Layered Cupcakes with Mocha Buttercream

This recipe makes six cupcakes for two dessert servings, and one extra to share later! You can easily multiply this recipe by two or four if you are baking for a larger group.

Makes 6 cupcakes for 3 servings

FOR THE CUPCAKES

⅔ cup sifted all-purpose flour

¼ teaspoon baking soda

⅛ teaspoon salt

4 tablespoons unsalted butter

⅔ cup sugar

1 large egg

½ teaspoon pure vanilla extract

⅓ cup whole milk

1 tablespoon coffee, cooled

¼ cup sifted cocoa powder

FOR THE MOCHA BUTTERCREAM FROSTING

8 tablespoons unsalted butter

2 cups sifted confectioners' sugar

½ teaspoon whole milk

¼ teaspoon salt

2 tablespoons coffee, cooled

FOR SERVING

1 tablespoon espresso powder

4 chocolate-covered espresso beans

For the cupcakes:

❶ Preheat the oven to 350°F. Line one cupcake pan with six paper baking cups.

❷ Sift together the flour, baking soda, and salt in a bowl, and set aside.

❸ Place the butter in the bowl of a stand mixer or in a bowl with a handheld electric mixer. Beat on medium speed until light and fluffy. Stop to add the sugar; then beat on medium speed until well incorporated, approximately 3 to 5 minutes. Add the egg, mixing slowly after it is added.

❹ Combine the vanilla extract, milk, and coffee in a large liquid measuring cup.

5 Add one third of the flour mixture to the butter mixture, then gradually add one third of the milk mixture, beating slowly until well incorporated. Add another third of the flour mixture, followed by another third of the milk mixture. Stop to scrape down the bowl as needed. Add the remaining flour mixture, followed by the remaining milk mixture, and mix slowly until just combined.

6 Add the cocoa powder, mixing on low speed until just incorporated.

7 Using a standard-size ice cream scoop, fill each baking cup so that it is two-thirds full. Bake for 14 to 16 minutes (start checking at 14 minutes) or until a toothpick inserted into the center of a cupcake comes out clean. Transfer the pan to a wire rack to cool completely.

For the frosting:

In the bowl of a stand mixer or in a bowl with a handheld electric mixer, combine all the ingredients and mix at high speed for 3 to 5 minutes, or until the frosting is light and airy.

To assemble:

Once the cupcakes have cooled, remove them from their wrappers. Place one cupcake in the bottom of a glass mug or a deep ice cream dish, and add a dollop of frosting on top. Then follow with another cupcake, and add a second dollop of frosting on top. Using a strainer, dust with a small amount of espresso powder. Add a chocolate-covered espresso bean on top, serve, and enjoy!

Whole Wheat Cranberry Orange Cupcakes

There is something extra special about being surprised with breakfast in bed. These cranberry orange cupcakes with an orange citrus glaze are the perfect way to surprise your sweetheart on a lazy Sunday morning, and the rest of the family will definitely enjoy them, too. If you don't like whole wheat flour, you can easily substitute regular all-purpose flour.

Makes 12 cupcakes

FOR THE CUPCAKES

2 cups sifted whole wheat flour

2½ teaspoons baking powder

½ teaspoon salt

8 tablespoons unsalted butter

¾ cup sugar

2 large eggs

1 cup whole milk

1 tablespoon freshly grated orange zest

1½ cups fresh cranberries (you can substitute frozen, if necessary)

FOR THE ORANGE CITRUS GLAZE

1¼ cups sifted confectioners' sugar

½ teaspoon freshly grated orange zest

3 tablespoons freshly squeezed orange juice

¼ teaspoon pure vanilla extract

For the cupcakes:

1 Preheat the oven to 350°F. Line a cupcake pan with twelve paper baking cups.

2 Sift together the flour, baking powder, and salt in a bowl, and set aside.

3 In the bowl of a stand mixer or in a bowl with a handheld electric mixer, cream together the butter and sugar for 3 to 5 minutes, or until light and fluffy.

4 Slowly add the eggs, mixing after each addition.

5 Add one third of the flour mixture to the butter mixture, followed by one third of the milk. Mix slowly. Add another third of the flour mixture, followed by another third of the milk. Mix again slowly. Add the final third of the flour mixture, followed by the final third of the milk. Mix slowly, stopping to scrape down the bowl.

6 Add the orange zest and mix until completely incorporated.

7 Using a spatula, gently fold in the cranberries.

8 Using a standard-size ice cream scoop, fill each baking cup so that it is two-thirds full, and bake for 22 to 24 minutes or until a toothpick inserted comes out clean.

For the glaze:

Whisk together all the ingredients in a small bowl, and warm in a small saucepan on low heat, stirring until fully mixed. Let the glaze cool for 10 minutes before drizzling on the cupcakes.

Serve in a lined basket, and enjoy for a delicious breakfast!

CHAPTER 5

Baby Showers

My Gifts from God (by Mommy)

When I found out I was pregnant with Sophie, it seemed like a miracle. I had tried for six years to have a baby, so I was over the moon. I had been waiting all my life for this day. God had answered my prayers, and I was finally pregnant!

My pregnancy with Sophie was difficult from the beginning. She was born six weeks premature and weighed only three and a half pounds. She was in the hospital for six weeks, and I was so happy the day I was able to take her home. I still remember it like it was yesterday. Sophie was my gift from God, and I felt so blessed and lucky to have such a sweet baby.

Since it was very difficult for me to get pregnant with Sophie, I believed that she would be my only child. When I found out, a year and a half later, that I was five months pregnant with Katherine, you can imagine how floored I was!

"Me? Pregnant? You have to be kidding me!" I told the doctor. How could I have not known that I was over five months along? I didn't lose my baby weight from Sophie, but still it was shocking for me to hear this news.

My second pregnancy was a lot easier, and when I went into labor the nurses asked me if I wanted a boy or a girl. I told them I wanted a boy, so the nurses had all these blue blankets ready. When Katherine was born, I was so excited to have another daughter—but poor Katherine got wrapped in the blue blankets in the operating room! I still remember that day, March 13, 1979, sitting on the hospital bed with Sophie, who was

Mommy and newborn baby Sophie.

Mommy, Sophie, and Katherine in the hospital the day Katherine was born.

just eighteen months old, while I held Katherine in my arms. I had never been happier in my life. Not much has changed since then! We are still all together and very close. I am so thankful to have the most amazing daughters who still want me in their lives.

Some people like to call me a baby pusher. I'm known for constantly pressuring Sophie and Katherine to have a baby. I can't help it if I'm a grandma-wannabe! Having a baby is the most amazing experience that a woman can have in life, and I can't wait for Sophie and Katherine to be mommies, too (hear that, girls?).

It's a Greek custom for family and friends to deliver a special treat when visiting a new baby: *tiganites,* which are bite-size, fat, sugary pancakes that are both fluffy and crispy. They are made with soda water, so they're puffy, and are fried in oil (instead of butter, like a pancake) and dusted with granulated sugar (instead of confectioners' sugar). You can also put syrup over them, but I like them with just a hint of sweetness on top.

—*Mommy*

Sophie, Mommy, and Katherine in 2007.

Tiganites (Sweet Pancake Medallions) It is a Greek tradition
to make these sweet pancake medallions when a new baby is born—they symbolize
good luck!

Makes 10 to 12 medallions

2 cups sifted all-purpose flour

1 teaspoon baking powder

¼ teaspoon salt

¼ teaspoon pure vanilla extract

1 cup whole milk

2 large eggs

¼ cup olive oil, plus additional to fry pancakes

juice of 1 small lemon

¼ cup 7-Up or Sprite soda (or any other soda
   water or lemon-lime soft drink)

granulated sugar for sprinkling

❶ Combine the flour, baking powder, and salt in the bowl of a stand mixer or in a bowl with a handheld electric mixer.

❷ In a separate bowl, combine the vanilla extract and milk.

❸ Add the milk mixture to the flour mixture, and mix together on medium speed until well combined.

❹ Separate the egg yolks from the egg whites. Add the egg yolks to the mixture, mixing on medium speed until just combined. Then lightly beat the egg whites and add to the mixture, mixing on low speed until just combined.

❺ Add ¼ cup olive oil and the lemon juice and soda to the mixture. Mix on medium speed until well combined.

❻ Pour additional olive oil into a deep frying pan until the layer of oil is ¼ inch deep.

❼ Heat frying pan to medium heat.

8 Pour a half-ladle-full of pancake mixture onto the frying pan, and fry for one minute on each side (until you see bubbles and browning on the sides). Then flip the pancakes *away* from you, so you don't get splashed with hot oil.

9 Place the cooked pancakes on a plate covered with a paper towel to absorb the oil.

10 Sprinkle granulated sugar over the hot pancakes to add a nice flavor and crunch. Serve and enjoy!

Yellow Ducky Cupcakes with Baby Blue and Baby Pink Buttercream Filling

Though we don't have any babies of our own yet, we absolutely love doing cupcakes for baby showers. One of our favorites is the "reveal" cupcake, which gives the mom-to-be a fun way to announce whether she is having a boy or a girl. When guests bite into their cupcakes, they're surprised with a filling of either baby pink or baby blue buttercream.

Makes 18 cupcakes

FOR THE CUPCAKES

2½ cups sifted all-purpose flour

½ teaspoon baking powder

¼ teaspoon salt

8 tablespoons unsalted butter

1¾ cups sugar

2 large eggs

2 large egg yolks

1¼ cups whole milk

2¼ teaspoons pure vanilla extract

FOR THE PASTEL-COLORED VANILLA BUTTERCREAM FROSTING

16 tablespoons unsalted butter

4 cups sifted confectioners' sugar

1 teaspoon pure vanilla extract

1 teaspoon whole milk

⅛ teaspoon salt

½ teaspoon blue or red gel food color

FOR THE DECORATION

¼ pound each yellow, orange, and blue fondant

piping gel

For the cupcakes:

1 Preheat the oven to 350°F. Line a cupcake pan with twelve paper baking cups and a second pan with six baking cups.

2 Sift together the flour, baking powder, and salt in a bowl, and set aside.

3 In the bowl of a stand mixer or in a bowl with a handheld electric mixer, cream together the butter and sugar until light and fluffy, approximately 3 to 5 minutes.

4 Add the eggs and egg yolks slowly, one at a time, mixing on low speed after each addition.

5 In a separate bowl, add the vanilla extract to the milk, and set aside.

6 Add one third of the flour mixture to the butter mixture. Mix on low speed. Add one third of the milk mixture, and mix on low speed. Add another third of the flour mixture, and mix on low speed. Add another third of the milk mixture, and mix on low speed. Finally, add the remaining flour mixture, mixing on low speed, followed by the remaining milk mixture, mixing on low speed until just incorporated.

7 Use a spatula to scrape down the sides of the mixing bowl.

8 Using a standard-size ice cream scoop, fill each baking cup so it is two-thirds full.

9 Bake for 15 to 18 minutes or until a toothpick inserted into the center of a cupcake comes out clean. Let the cupcakes cool on a wire rack for approximately 20 minutes.

For the frosting:

1 Add the butter, sugar, vanilla extract, milk, and salt to the bowl of a stand mixer or a bowl with a handheld electric mixer, and mix on high speed until light and airy, approximately 3 to 5 minutes.

2 Remove one quarter of the frosting from the bowl of the mixer and place it in a smaller bowl.

3 To the frosting in the smaller bowl, add the red or blue food color, and mix until your desired shade of pink or blue is achieved.

4 Using an apple corer, remove the centers of each of your cupcakes. Fill a piping bag with the pink or blue frosting, and pipe it into the center of each cupcake.

5 Then frost the top of each cupcake with a signature swirl (see page xxv) of the plain frosting.

To make the fondant duckies:

This cute fondant topper in the shape of a darling rubber ducky will delight your shower guests! Break off a piece of yellow fondant roughly the size of a walnut. Pinch off about a third and roll into a ball. This will be the head of your duck. Shape the other two thirds into a crescent shape. This will be the body of your duck. Using piping gel or water, attach the ball to the crescent. Then take a piece of orange fondant the size of a pea, and form the bill of your duck. Using piping gel or water, attach the bill to the duck's head. Finally, take two tiny pieces of blue fondant, and place them on the duck's head as eyes. Place on top of a cupcake, and repeat for all your cupcakes.

Part 2

....

HOLIDAYS

These are the days to celebrate with family and friends and relax, reflect, and give thanks for all of life's sweet moments.

CHAPTER 6

New Year's Eve

A Greek New Year's Eve

Do you remember December 31, 1999 . . . the start of the twenty-first century and the 2000s? We were both in college, at home for our winter break, and we wanted to celebrate the new Y2K with some old traditions as well. Most people our age liked to get dressed up for wild nights at clubs on New Year's Eve, but not us. We preferred to stay home with family, gather around the table, and share small plates of food—or meze, as they're called in the Greek culture. For this momentous New Year's Eve, we wanted to surprise our family and prepare everything ourselves. We shooed Mommy out of the kitchen and dining room and got down to work!

We set the table with Mommy's best tablecloth and all her good china and crystal. We bought colorful "2000" party hats for everyone and placed one at each place setting. We scattered glittery confetti all over the table, so that it glistened under the light. We blew up colorful metallic balloons and anchored them to the ceiling. We had a lot of family coming over—a dozen or so of our aunts, uncles, and cousins—so there was definitely a lot to do and a lot of meze plates to prepare.

There are certain meze staples in the Greek culture that you just need to have on the table no matter what the occasion: black olives, feta cheese, roasted red peppers, bread, and olive oil. These were a given. But we also whipped up tomato bruschetta, stuffed mushroom caps, sautéed scallops, and breaded feta cheese cubes—one of our personal favorites. It's the Greek version of the Italian breaded mozzarella stick.

Part of the fun for us was continually arranging these meze on platters and ferrying them to the table all night. We felt like we were working at a real catering company—making sure all the plates were replenished and everyone's glass was full. By the time the clock struck midnight, we were exhausted. But now it was time for dessert!

Every New Year's, Babee would make a traditional Greek pastry called *vasilopita,* aka St. Basil's cake, as January 1 is also known as the day of St. Basil the Great. Following Greek tradition, Babee would place a foil-wrapped coin inside the *vasilopita.* Whoever finds the coin is supposed to have good luck for the entire year. So of course we wanted to continue this tradition, and placed a foil-wrapped coin inside our batter. While the *vasilopita* was baking, we reset the table for dessert: honey, nuts, fresh fruit, and some of Babee's famous marble cake, cut into small squares. These are all Greek symbols of happiness.

Our oven timer went off just after midnight, and we took out the *vasilopita* and placed it on the table, still warm. Our dad cut it for everyone in a special order: the first piece was for St. Basil, the second for our house, and then by age. When we were younger, Babee would always plant two coins in the cake and make sure that each of us got one.

But tonight, it was completely up to fate. We all took a bite, hoping for the coin, and it was Mommy who shouted, "I got it!" We cheered and hugged her. Then she broke her piece of cake in two and gave each of us part of it—so we could all share in the good luck of the new millennium.

Recipe for Success

The Perfect Toast

$\mathcal{W}$e've all been there: parties or events where somebody gives a toast that seems to last forever. At a party, everyone wants to party—not listen to a lecture. So if you're the person who's doing the talking, here's some advice:

• **Keep it short and sweet.** Some of the most memorable toasts are just a sentence or two. At Katherine's wedding, our dad famously spent five minutes searching in his tuxedo pocket for his notes, and then when he retrieved them, his toast was seven words long: "Katherine and Ben, we love you! Congratulations!" Everyone laughed hysterically and loved it.

• **Write down your thoughts in advance,** and think hard about the main message you want to get across.

• **Choose your words carefully,** and keep your toast to no longer than two minutes. That way your message won't get lost on guests, and it will have more impact.

• **When you're done,** raise your glass high and wish your guests good health or good cheer—to seal the toast. In Greek we say *"Stin ygia mas!"* and in Hebrew it's *"L'chaim!"*

Greek Vasilopita (New Year's Cake)

Makes one 9-inch round cake

2½ cups sifted all-purpose flour

1 teaspoon baking powder

16 tablespoons unsalted butter

1½ cups sugar

6 large eggs

1 cup whole milk

1 teaspoon freshly grated lemon zest

1 quarter wrapped in foil

confectioners' sugar, for dusting

❶ Preheat the oven to 350°F. Grease a round 9-inch cake pan with butter.

❷ Sift together the flour and baking powder, and set aside.

❸ In the bowl of a stand mixer or in a bowl with a handheld electric mixer, cream together the butter and sugar until light and fluffy, approximately 3 to 5 minutes.

❹ Add the eggs slowly, one by one, mixing after each addition.

❺ Heat milk in the microwave for 1 minute to warm.

❻ Add a third of the flour mixture to the butter mixture, followed by a third of the milk, mixing slowly after each addition. Next, add another third of the flour mixture, followed by another third of the milk, mixing slowly after each addition. Finally, add the remaining flour mixture, followed by the remaining milk, and mix until just combined. Stop to scrape down the bowl as needed.

❼ Add the lemon zest, and mix until just incorporated.

❽ Pour the batter into the cake pan. Place the wrapped coin somewhere in the batter.

9 Bake for 45 minutes or until a toothpick inserted comes out clean. Transfer the pan to a wire rack to cool completely.

10 Dust with confectioners' sugar, serve, and may the lucky person find the coin!

Chocolate Salted Caramel Pop Rocks Cupcakes

If you want to serve a New Year's Eve dessert with an extra-special celebratory spark and pop, this recipe is great! It's a twist on our Strawberry Champagne Sparkler cupcakes—we serve it in champagne flutes, too. When your guests take a bite, there will definitely be a party in their mouths. Just be sure to wait until the last moment to add the Pop Rocks, because as soon as they hit a wet surface, they will lose their fizzle! We also like to add a jagged piece of edible gold leaf on top to give each cupcake a little extra bling.

Serves 12 people (36 mini cupcakes, 3 per champagne flute)

FOR THE CUPCAKES

1¼ cups sifted all-purpose flour

½ teaspoon baking soda

¼ teaspoon salt

8 tablespoons unsalted butter

1¼ cups sugar

2 large eggs

1¼ teaspoons pure vanilla extract

1 cup whole milk

½ cup sifted cocoa powder

FOR THE CARAMEL

Makes 2½ cups caramel

2 cups sugar

1 tablespoon water

12 tablespoons unsalted butter

1 teaspoon pure vanilla extract

1 cup heavy cream

FOR THE SALTED CARAMEL BUTTERCREAM FROSTING

16 tablespoons unsalted butter

4 cups sifted confectioners' sugar

1 teaspoon whole milk

1 teaspoon pure vanilla extract

1 teaspoon salt

FOR SERVING

12 glass champagne flutes

1½ cups chocolate-covered Pop Rocks candy

12 small pieces of edible gold leaf (optional)

12 long spoons

For the cupcakes:

1 Preheat the oven to 350°F. Line one mini cupcake pan with twenty-four mini paper baking cups and a second mini cupcake pan with twelve baking cups.

2 Sift together the flour, baking soda, and salt in a bowl, and set aside.

3 Place the butter in the bowl of a stand mixer or in a bowl with a handheld electric mixer. Add the sugar; beat on medium speed until well incorporated, approximately 3 to 5 minutes.

4 Add the eggs one at a time, mixing slowly after each addition.

5 Combine the vanilla extract and milk in a large liquid measuring cup.

6 Add one third of the flour mixture to the butter mixture, then gradually add one third of the milk mixture, beating slowly until well incorporated. Add another third of the flour mixture, followed by another third of the milk mixture. Stop to scrape down the bowl as needed. Add the remaining flour mixture, followed by the remaining milk mixture, and beat just until combined.

7 Add the cocoa powder, mixing on low speed just until incorporated.

8 Scoop batter into baking cups so that each is two-thirds full, and bake for 10 minutes or until a toothpick inserted into the center of a cupcake comes out clean. Transfer the pans to a wire rack to cool completely. If using paper baking cups, peel off all of the baking cups from the cupcakes.

For the caramel:

1 Pour the sugar and water into a large saucepan and warm on medium-high heat. Stir constantly until the sugar completely liquefies. Be careful not to burn the sugar.

2 After all the sugar has dissolved, add the butter and vanilla extract to the saucepan and mix thoroughly.

3 Once the butter has melted and the butter and sugar are completely mixed, remove from heat and, using a whisk, slowly beat in the heavy cream until the mixture is a beautiful golden brown caramel color.

4 Set aside to let cool and thicken for 5 minutes at room temperature. Then refrigerate for at least 20 minutes to thicken further before using.

For the frosting:

1 Place all of the ingredients and ½ cup of the caramel in the bowl of a stand mixer or in a bowl with a handheld electric mixer, and mix on high speed until well incorporated and the frosting is light and airy.

2 Place the frosting in a disposable piping bag with a large round metal tip.

To assemble the layers in champagne flutes:

Line up twelve glass champagne flutes. Insert one mini chocolate cupcake in the bottom of each glass. Next, pipe a swirl of frosting on top of each cupcake. Add a swirl of the remaining caramel and a spoonful of the chocolate Pop Rocks. Repeat layers. Finally, place a third mini chocolate cupcake at the top of each glass, pipe with a Georgetown Cupcake signature swirl (see page xxv) of frosting, top with a final spoonful of Pop Rocks, and garnish with a jagged piece of gold leaf, if desired. Serve with spoons at midnight, and enjoy!

CHAPTER 7

Valentine's Day

Be My Valentine

For our Valentine's Day parties at our elementary school, Babee helped us make her famous shortbread cookies with strawberry preserve filling. The cookies were round, and our favorite part of them was the circular "window" in the front that allowed us to peek at the strawberry filling inside. Sometimes we took a big bite of the cookie sandwich. Other times we twisted them apart and licked out the filling separately. Babee's cookie jar was always full of these scrumptious treats, and everyone was obsessed with them. They were legendary. Our cousins would run over just to raid Babee's cookie jar!

We had so much fun baking the cookies, and we were so proud to carry them to school the next day for our parties. Everyone else was giving out paper Valentines, but ours were edible—definitely the biggest hit!

Strawberry Shortcake Cupcakes

This cupcake is a twist on Babee's strawberry shortbread cookies, and is the perfect dessert for a Valentine's Day party or a romantic dinner for two! The filling can be prepared the night before and stored in the refrigerator.

Makes 24 cupcakes

FOR THE VANILLA CREME FILLING

2 large egg yolks

¼ cup sugar

¼ cup sifted all-purpose flour

¼ cup cornstarch

1 cup whole milk

2 tablespoons heavy cream

¼ teaspoon rum extract

1 teaspoon pure vanilla extract

seeds from 1 vanilla bean

FOR THE CUPCAKES

2½ cups sifted all-purpose flour

2½ teaspoons baking powder

¼ teaspoon salt

8 tablespoons unsalted butter

1¾ cups sugar

2 large eggs

2¼ teaspoons pure vanilla extract

1¼ cups whole milk

seeds from 1 vanilla bean

1 cup fresh strawberries, diced

FOR THE FROSTING

16 tablespoons unsalted butter

4 cups sifted confectioners' sugar

1 teaspoon whole milk

1 teaspoon pure vanilla extract

¼ teaspoon salt

½ cup diced strawberries

24 fresh strawberries, sliced, for inside layer and garnish

For the filling:

❶ In the bowl of a stand mixer, using the paddle attachment, or in a bowl with a handheld electric mixer, mix the egg yolks and the sugar for 4 to 5 minutes.

2 In another large bowl, sift together the flour and the cornstarch.

3 Add the flour mixture to the egg mixture slowly, mixing on low speed for 1 to 2 minutes or until smooth.

4 In a medium saucepan, warm the milk on medium heat, just until it starts to boil.

5 Switch your mixer to the whisk attachment, then add the hot milk slowly to the mixer, and whisk continuously at medium speed while pouring the milk, to keep the mixture smooth, without lumps or curdles.

6 Add the heavy cream, rum extract, vanilla extract, and vanilla bean seeds and mix thoroughly for 2 to 3 minutes.

7 Then pour the mixture back into the saucepan and cook over medium heat until it boils. Note: It must be hand-whisked constantly during this time. After it reaches boiling, whisk for 2 more minutes, until it thickens.

8 Remove from heat. Let it come to room temperature before pouring in a bowl. Refrigerate for at least 2 hours to chill.

For the cupcakes:

1 Preheat the oven to 350°F. Line two cupcake pans with twelve paper baking cups each, or grease pans with butter if not using baking cups.

2 Sift together the flour, baking powder, and salt in a bowl, and set aside.

3 Place the butter in the bowl of a stand mixer or in a bowl with a handheld electric mixer. Add the sugar; beat on medium speed until well incorporated, approximately 3 to 5 minutes.

4 Add the eggs one at a time, mixing slowly after each addition.

5 Combine the vanilla extract and milk in a large liquid measuring cup. Carefully scrape the vanilla bean seeds into the milk.

6 Add one third of the flour mixture to the butter mixture, then gradually add one third of the milk mixture, beating slowly until well incorporated. Add another third of the flour mixture, followed by another third of the milk mixture. Stop to scrape down the bowl as needed. Add the remaining flour mixture, followed by the remaining milk mixture, and beat just until combined.

7 Using a spatula, gently fold in the strawberries.

8 Scoop batter into baking cups so that each is two-thirds full, and bake for 15 to 18 minutes or until a toothpick inserted into the center of a cupcake comes out clean. Transfer the pans to a wire rack to cool completely.

For the frosting:

Place all of the ingredients in the bowl of a stand mixer or in a bowl with a handheld electric mixer. Beat until well incorporated and the frosting is light and fluffy, approximately 3 to 4 minutes.

To assemble:

Once cooled, peel the wrappers off the strawberry cupcakes and slice in half lengthwise. Add a tablespoon of the filling on top of the bottom half of the strawberry cupcake; add a layer of sliced strawberries; cover with the top to make a cupcake "sandwich"; then frost with a signature swirl (see page xxv) and garnish with a strawberry slice.

Babee's Strawberry Shortbread Valentine's Cookies

Makes 6 to 8 dozen cookies (depending on size)

6 cups sifted all-purpose flour

1 teaspoon baking powder

2 cups unsalted butter

2 cups sifted confectioners' sugar

2 large egg yolks

½ cup orange juice

1 teaspoon pure vanilla extract

6 cups strawberry preserves

1 Preheat the oven to 350°F. Sift together the flour and baking powder, and set aside.

2 In the bowl of a stand mixer or in a bowl with a handheld electric mixer, cream together the butter and sugar until light and fluffy, approximately 3 to 5 minutes.

3 Add the egg yolks, orange juice, and vanilla extract, and mix slowly.

4 Add the flour mixture to the butter mixture, and mix slowly until a dough forms.

5 Remove the dough from the mixer, and knead with your hands until it's stretchy. Place the dough between two sheets of parchment paper and, using a rolling pin, roll flat.

6 Remove the top sheet of parchment paper and cut the dough in half. Punch out the "solid" bottom halves of the cookies on one half of the dough. Punch out the "heart window" top halves of the cookies on the other half of the dough.

7 Arrange cookies on a cookie sheet lined with parchment paper and bake for 8 to 10 minutes. Remove before browned, and let cool completely.

8 Carefully spread strawberry preserves on the solid bottom halves of the cookies, and place the heart window part of each cookie on top. Serve and enjoy!

CHAPTER ⊚ 8

Easter

A Traditional Easter

When we were little, we had a huge Easter celebration with our family every year. Preparations always began the day before: our dad went to the local butcher and picked out a huge lamb, while we joined Babee and Mommy in the kitchen. Everyone had a task: Mommy made spinach and feta cheese rolls, while Babee baked her traditional Easter bread. Our job was to hard-boil Easter eggs and then color them, mostly in a deep red like most Greek households did, for the Easter egg hunt the following day. We would also get creative and make some multicolored ones, drawing on the shells with brightly colored crayons and then dipping them into beautiful pastel food color.

We also made our own Easter baskets from the materials Mommy picked up at the craft store: woven baskets, flowers, colored paper, markers, and shiny, velvety fabric.

We had a contest to see who could make the most beautiful basket, while Babee would start to scope out the best hiding places for the Easter eggs and other treats. Sometimes we followed her around as she did this, hoping to sneak a peek at her potential hiding places, while she pretended not to notice us.

On Easter morning, we slept in after the long night at church, then came downstairs for breakfast in our brand-new dresses. At our place settings at the table, Babee loaded our colorful Easter baskets with huge chocolate Easter bunnies and other goodies. After breakfast (and filling up on cookies and chocolate!), we grabbed our Easter baskets and went hunting for eggs, trying to guess where Babee had placed them. We started inside the house, peering inside desk drawers, on windowsills, and behind table legs. Then we raced outside to scour the yard for little wrapped presents and candies. We ran around for hours while Babee smiled at us from the front porch.

Babee always knew how to make Easter a fun and interactive celebration for us, and her attention to every detail is the same approach that we take to creating cupcake assortments and displays for beautiful celebrations at Georgetown Cupcake.

making your own easter basket cupcake wrappers

If you want to dress up your cupcakes for an Easter party, make these fun cupcake wrappers to place around your cupcakes! What you'll need:

- Pastel-colored or patterned scrapbook paper

- Decorative paper punch (in a small pattern)

- Scissors

- Glue stick

Cut the scrapbook paper into a rectangular piece 2 inches wide by 8 inches long. Using a decorative paper punch in the pattern of your choice, punch along one edge of the rectangle. Glue along the end of the back of one side to form a ring, making it slightly narrower at the bottom.

Cut another strip ½ inch wide by 6 inches long. Place a small dab of glue on the front side of each end, and glue onto the basket to form the handle. Place the paper basket on top of a cupcake.

Repeat for each cupcake, mixing and matching the paper for the baskets and the handles. Serve, and delight your guests! ✳

Almond Easter Bunny Cupcakes

Makes 24 cupcakes

2½ cups sifted all-purpose flour

2½ teaspoons baking powder

¼ teaspoon salt

8 tablespoons unsalted butter

1¾ cups sugar

2 large eggs

2 large egg yolks

1¼ cups whole milk

2¼ teaspoons pure almond extract

FOR THE FROSTING

16 tablespoons unsalted butter

4 cups sifted confectioners' sugar

1 teaspoon whole milk

1 teaspoon pure vanilla extract

⅛ teaspoon salt

FOR THE DECORATION

¼ pound each lavender, purple, white, and pink
   fondant

piping gel

For the cupcakes:

❶ Preheat the oven to 350°F. Line two cupcake pans with twelve paper baking cups each.

❷ Sift together the flour, baking powder, and salt in a bowl, and set aside.

❸ In the bowl of a stand mixer or in a bowl with a handheld electric mixer, cream together the butter and sugar on medium speed until light and fluffy, approximately 3 to 5 minutes.

❹ Add the eggs and egg yolks one at a time, mixing slowly after each addition.

❺ Combine the milk and almond extract in a large liquid measuring cup.

6 Add one third of the flour mixture to the butter mixture, then gradually add one third of the milk mixture, beating slowly until well incorporated. Add another third of the flour mixture, followed by another third of the milk mixture. Stop to scrape down the bowl as needed. Add the remaining flour mixture, followed by the remaining milk mixture, and beat just until combined.

7 Scoop batter into baking cups so that each is two-thirds full, and bake for 15 to 18 minutes or until a toothpick inserted into the center of a cupcake comes out clean. Transfer the pans to a wire rack to cool completely.

For the frosting:

1 Place all of the ingredients in the bowl of a stand mixer or in a bowl with a hand-held electric mixer. Beat until well incorporated and the frosting is light and fluffy, approximately 3 to 5 minutes.

2 Frost each cupcake with Georgetown Cupcake's signature swirl (see page xxv).

To make the fondant Easter bunnies:

1 Roll out a piece of lavender fondant, and using a cookie cutter, cut out two circles with a diameter of 3 inches each.

2 Lay one circle flat on your work surface to form the bunny's face.

3 Using the same cookie cutter, cut approximately ½ inch off the sides of the second circle to form the bunny's ears.

4 Roll out a piece of pink fondant, and using a cookie cutter, cut out one circle with a diameter of approximately 1½ inches.

5 Using the same cookie cutter, cut approximately ¼ inch off the sides of the circle to form the insides of the bunny's ears.

6 Using piping gel or water, attach the pink inner ears to the purple outer ears. Then attach the completed bunny's ears to the top of the large lavender circle using piping gel or water.

7 Roll out a small ball of pink fondant, approximately the size of a pea, and flatten the top and bottom to form the bunny's nose. Place it in the center of the bunny's face, attaching it with piping gel or water.

8 Roll out two small balls of white fondant, each approximately the size of a pea, and flatten.

9 Roll out two small balls of purple fondant, each approximately the size of half a pea. Using piping gel or water, attach the purple fondant balls to the white fondant circles to form the bunny's eyes. Also using piping gel or water, attach the bunny's eyes to its face so that they are centered and equally spaced above the pink nose.

10 Roll out a piece of white fondant, and using a scalpel, carefully cut out two small rectangles, ¼ inch tall by ⅛ inch wide. Using piping gel or water, attach these white rectangles side-by-side under the bunny's nose to form the teeth.

11 Let the completed bunny's face lie flat to set for 5 to 10 minutes, and then place the bunny face on top of cupcake. Serve and enjoy!

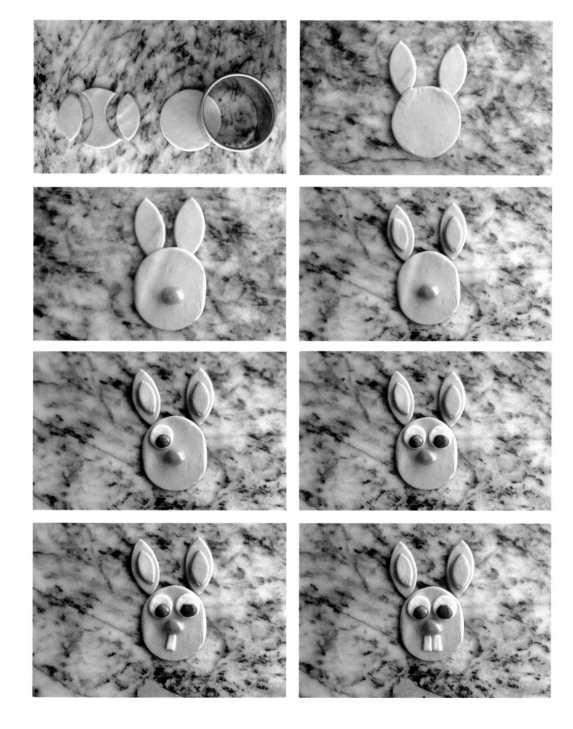

White Chocolate Mini Egg Cupcakes in Egg Cartons

These cupcakes have a chocolate base studded with white chocolate chips and are topped with a white chocolate buttercream. They remind us of chocolate and white chocolate Easter bunnies!

Makes 48 mini cupcakes (to fill 4 egg cartons)

FOR THE CUPCAKES

1¼ cups sifted all-purpose flour

½ teaspoon baking soda

¼ teaspoon salt

8 tablespoons unsalted butter

1¼ cups sugar

2 large eggs

1¼ teaspoons pure vanilla extract

1 cup whole milk

½ cup sifted cocoa powder

2 cups white chocolate chips

FOR THE FROSTING

16 tablespoons unsalted butter

4 cups sifted confectioners' sugar

1 teaspoon whole milk

1 teaspoon pure vanilla extract

¼ teaspoon salt

½ cup white chocolate chips, melted

FOR THE DECORATION

¼ pound fondant in each of your favorite
    pastel colors

¼ cup each cupcake toppings of your choice,
    or gel food color and a brush

4 empty egg cartons

For the cupcakes:

❶ Preheat the oven to 350°F. Line two mini cupcake pans with twenty-four paper baking cups each.

❷ Sift together the flour, baking soda, and salt in a bowl, and set aside.

❸ Place the butter in the bowl of a stand mixer or in a bowl with a handheld electric mixer. Add the sugar; beat on medium speed until well incorporated.

4 Add the eggs one at a time, mixing slowly after each addition.

5 Combine the vanilla extract and milk in a large liquid measuring cup.

6 Add one third of the flour mixture to the butter mixture, then gradually add one third of the milk mixture, beating slowly until well incorporated. Add another third of the flour mixture, followed by another third of the milk mixture. Stop to scrape down the bowl as needed. Add the remaining flour mixture, followed by the remaining milk mixture, and beat just until combined.

7 Add the cocoa powder, and mix until just combined.

8 Mix in the white chocolate chips until just combined.

9 Scoop batter into baking cups so that each is two-thirds full, and bake for 10 to 12 minutes or until a toothpick inserted into the center of a cupcake comes out clean. Transfer the pans to a wire rack to cool completely.

For the frosting:

1 Place all of the ingredients in the bowl of a stand mixer or in a bowl with a hand-held electric mixer. Beat until well incorporated and the frosting is light and fluffy, approximately 3 to 5 minutes.

2 Frost each of your cupcakes using the signature swirl (see page xxv).

To make the fondant Easter eggs:

1 Roll out pieces of fondant and cut them into egg shapes. Decorate the eggs with cupcake toppings, or use a small brush to paint line patterns of food color on the eggs.

2 Nestle an egg on top of each cupcake. Place twelve cupcakes in each egg carton, and serve!

no piping bag, no problem!

In a hurry to decorate some cupcakes, but have no piping tips or bags on hand? No worries—you can decorate your cupcakes with the help of just a regular zip-lock bag! For example, to pipe the carrot shown in the photo below, simply snip a corner off two plastic sandwich or freezer bags about a quarter inch from the tip of the bag, so that there is a small opening at the corner of each bag. Using a back-and-forth zigzag motion, squeeze orange icing on top of your cupcake to create the shape of a carrot, starting wide at the top and narrowing your zigzag strokes as you get to the tip of the carrot. For the carrot stem, squeeze the green frosting in three or four broad strokes at the top of your carrot. How's that for improvising? ✱

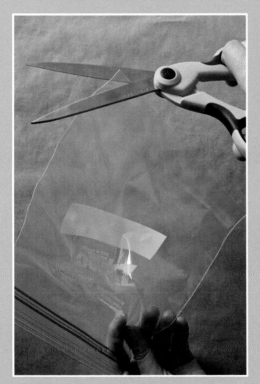

Babee's Koulourakia (Greek Butter Cookies) These traditional

Greek cookies are served at Easter and other major holidays. When stacked high with pastel-colored Easter eggs in a colorful Easter basket and wrapped with cellophane and a giant bow, they make the perfect item to bring to an Easter brunch.

Makes 40 to 50 cookies (depending on size)

32 tablespoons unsalted butter

1½ cups sugar

2 large eggs, plus 1 additional large egg for egg wash

2 tablespoons orange juice

1 teaspoon vanilla

2 teaspoons baking powder

4 cups sifted all-purpose flour

½ cup sesame seeds

1 Preheat the oven to 350°F, and grease a cookie sheet with butter or line it with parchment paper.

2 In the bowl of a stand mixer or in a bowl with a handheld electric mixer, cream together the butter and sugar at medium speed until light and fluffy, approximately 3 to 5 minutes.

3 Add the 2 eggs slowly, one at a time, mixing on low speed.

4 Add the orange juice and vanilla, and mix thoroughly.

5 Add the baking powder and flour slowly, mixing slowly until a thick dough forms.

6 Remove dough from mixer bowl and place it on top of a lightly floured surface. Knead the dough with your hands for 2 to 3 minutes, and let it sit for 10 to 15 minutes.

7 Take a small piece of dough the size of a golf ball and roll into a long strip. Fold the strip over and braid the dough into a twist, a wreath, or any other desired shape. Repeat until all the dough is used.

8 Beat the remaining egg for the egg wash, and brush the egg over the cookies. Sprinkle sesame seeds on top of each cookie.

9 Bake for 18 to 20 minutes. Transfer the cookies to a wire rack to cool completely.

10 Wrap the cookies with cellophane and a large pastel bow—this makes the perfect gift!

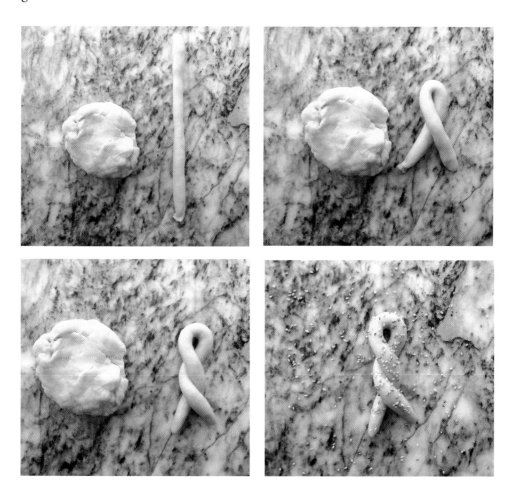

cupcake toppings 101

When you walk into the cake aisle of a specialty food store, are you overwhelmed by all the cupcake-decorating options? Jimmies versus dragées? Sanding sugar versus crystallized sugar? What are the differences between them? Which should you use for which occasion? Here's a quick guide to help you distinguish between nonpareils and pailletés!

Jimmies These sprinkles are the most traditional cupcake decorations. They have a long, narrow shape and come in a wide variety of colors, including rainbow. They have a more casual and nostalgic feel. We reserve them for kids' cupcakes and casual-themed birthdays.

Sanding Sugar This is a fine-grain sugar with a shimmery texture that is available in a wide variety of colors. We find that it looks best when you cover the entire surface of your frosting with it, so that it is completely coated. It gives a cool texture. Clear sanding sugar looks fantastic on all frosting colors; we use colored sanding sugars only when we have a frosting in the exact same color. It's a perfect accent on cupcakes for fancier events like bridal showers, weddings, anniversaries, and evening parties.

Crystallized Sugar This is similar to sanding sugar, except that the grains are much coarser and look like tiny crystals. Like sanding sugar, crystallized sugar is available in a rainbow of colors. Because of its coarse texture we use this sparingly, sprinkling a small amount on top of our cupcakes. Unlike sanding sugar, we find that crystallized sugar looks best when you mix and match it with different frosting colors. It's very versatile, and we use it on cupcakes for casual and formal affairs alike.

Dragées Dragées are small metallic balls that come in gold, silver, pink, and teal, and in several different sizes. Be careful with these! Although they are beautiful to use as decorations, dragées should not be eaten. You can crack your teeth on them—trust us! We use dragées only as accents on our cupcakes—placing them strategically, using tweezers, since they are slippery to handle. Dragées, by nature, are very elegant and look beautiful. Because they should not be eaten, we use them sparingly—only for decorating cupcakes for formal affairs. Refrain from decorating kids' cupcakes with dragées!

Nonpareils These are round versions of jimmies. Like jimmies, they are available in a wide variety of colors including rainbow, which is our personal favorite! We like the round look of nonpareils and use them much more frequently than jimmies. They can be sprinkled on top of cupcakes liberally and are perfect for fun, casual parties.

Edible Confetti We like to think of confetti as the flattened cousin of the jimmies and nonpareils. Like its cousins, it comes in a wide variety of colors, including rainbow, and can be sprinkled on top of cupcakes for fun, casual parties.

Edible Pearls Edible pearls are similar to dragées, except that they have a pearlized texture and come in several different sizes. Be careful with these, too! Like dragées, they are beautiful to use as decorations, but some types are very hard; while they are technically edible, we don't recommend eating them. We use them only as accents. Tweezers are the best way to handle them. They are gorgeous, and we do use them strategically for decorating cupcakes for weddings and formal affairs. We do not recommend using them on kids' cupcakes.

Candied Flowers Candied rose and violet petals are beautiful accents to place on top of cupcakes. They tend to be quite pricey, so we use them sparingly. Candied flowers have a casual elegance, making them perfect for romantic or feminine parties such as bridal showers, tea parties, or brunches.

Chocolate Pailletés These are real chocolate sprinkles from France. They have a square shape and a beautiful shiny smooth texture! We have fallen in love with them, and they are the only type of chocolate sprinkles we use on our cupcakes. They are sometimes hard to find at the supermarket, but most specialty food stores have them. We use them to coat our chocolate cubed cupcakes and to sprinkle on our chocolate and vanilla cupcakes. They are very versatile and can be used for cupcakes for all types of occasions.

Gold Leaf This is definitely a way to give your cupcakes the Midas touch! Edible gold leaf is real gold, and it's safe to eat. You can break it up and place it on your cupcakes, or grind it into a fine powder and sprinkle it on. But don't go overboard, because this stuff is expensive. Gold leaf should be reserved for super-important occasions, such as weddings. You don't want to bring gold leaf cupcakes to your neighbor's potluck barbecue! ✪

CHAPTER 9

Passover

My First Seder

Passover is a special time for Jewish families and friends to get together and celebrate. The tradition of Passover marks the exodus of the Jews from Egypt in the time of Moses and centers on a special dinner called the Seder. During this meal, Jews reflect on why this night is different from all other nights. Passover is also important in the Christian religion since the Seder was "the Last Supper" leading up to the Easter holiday.

I had celebrated Passover in the past with my husband Ben's family, but this was the first time I planned to prepare the entire Seder dinner all by myself in our home. It was a huge undertaking, and I woke up at the crack of dawn to start cooking. It was important for me to take everything I had learned and studied in my Judaism classes and apply it. But to be honest, there were a few dishes of the Seder meal that were not exactly my favorite—namely the smelly gefilte fish! But I was determined to make and serve them all.

The first order of the day was to boil a big pot of water with fresh chicken, flavoring my stock for the matzo ball soup. Once the soup was boiling, I mixed matzo meal with eggs and formed the matzo balls with my hands. I dropped them in to simmer and watched as they immediately plumped up.

> *I took the golden brown macaroons out of the oven and drizzled melted ganache and caramel sauce over them.*

While the soup was cooking, I placed the whole chicken and vegetables in the oven to roast, and prepared the Seder plate. I went through the list of everything that needed to be on the plate: a lamb shank bone, bitter herbs, boiled egg, *charoset* (a mixture of apples, cinnamon, and chopped nuts), lettuce and parsley, and salt water. Each of these items symbolizes an important aspect of the Jews' exodus from Egypt. Seeing, smelling, and tasting these foods helps us "experience" what our ancestors went through. For example, bitter herbs remind us of the bitterness of slavery, charoset symbolizes the mortar used by Jewish slaves to build Egyptian buildings, and the salt water reminds us of the tears the Jews shed over their hardship.

Perhaps the most recognized food of all at the Seder table is the matzo, a flat unleavened square that is similar to a cracker. We eat matzo instead of bread for the entire week of Passover because it is what the Jews ate when they were fleeing Egypt. They were in such a hurry that they didn't have time to wait for their bread dough to rise. I placed three matzo on a plate and covered them with an embroidered matzo cover. During the dinner, we broke the middle matzo (called the *afikomen*), and my husband, Ben, placed it in a hiding place. According to tradition, the person who finds the afikomen wins a prize. This year, Mommy found it!

After the dinner (which everyone loved!), I slipped away during the conversation to start working on my dessert for the evening: coconut macaroons. Coconut macaroons are a great dessert for Passover because, as with bread, Jews can't eat cake on this special holiday. As I popped them in the oven, the kitchen quickly filled with the heavenly aroma of coconut toasting.

After thirty minutes, I took the golden brown macaroons out of the oven and drizzled melted ganache and caramel sauce over them. I served them to my guests as we chatted more about our history and future. I couldn't help smiling and feeling proud of myself; what a sweet ending to my first Seder!

—*Katherine*

Katherine's Passover Macaroons

Makes 12 large macaroons

seeds from 1 vanilla bean

¾ cup sweetened condensed milk

¼ teaspoon pure vanilla extract

2 large egg whites

¼ teaspoon salt

3 cups shredded coconut (sweetened if
  preferred)

½ cup Chocolate Ganache (page 7) or caramel
  (page 74)

1 Preheat the oven to 325°F, and line a baking sheet with parchment paper.

2 Scrape the vanilla bean seeds into the condensed milk. Add the vanilla extract to the condensed milk mixture, and stir until the seeds are well blended.

3 Pour the egg whites into a glass bowl and add the salt. Beat the egg whites on high speed using a handheld electric mixer until stiff peaks form.

4 Pour the coconut into a large bowl, and add the condensed milk mixture. Fold the mixture together.

5 Fold in the egg whites.

6 Using a standard-size ice cream scoop, scoop balls onto parchment paper.

7 Bake for 30 minutes or until macaroons are golden brown.

8 Drizzle ganache or caramel on top, and enjoy!

Be a Gracious Guest—Thank Your Host!

*S*ometimes what is even more important than being a good hostess is being a good guest. It's important to be gracious and say thank you for being invited to a party, especially at someone's home. The best and most memorable way to do this? Bring a hostess gift! It doesn't have to be expensive or fancy by any means. A dozen cupcakes gift-wrapped in a box make the perfect present. Give them to your hostess as you walk into the party, so she can serve them with dessert. A hostess gift shows that you care and does not go unnoticed.

CHAPTER 10

Mother's Day

A Blessing in Disguise

It was the scariest day of our lives: Mommy was being rushed to Virginia Hospital Center, and Ben and I were in our car, following closely behind the ambulance. Steve and Sophie were on their way as well. We had just finished filming interviews for an episode of *DC Cupcakes* when Mommy began to have trouble breathing and felt dizzy. This was totally unexpected because she is the one who's always talking and has the *most* energy of all of us! I knew something was very, very wrong and dialed 911, then prayed that everything was going to be okay.

As we arrived at the hospital, Mommy was in good spirits, as always. She was embarrassed by all the attention she was getting from the nice doctors and nurses, and kept telling everyone not to worry. She is a true Greek mother in that sense, always concerned about everyone else and never herself. The doctor checked her vital signs, but even though she now seemed fine, he wanted to figure out what had caused her breathing trouble. As I walked Mommy to the bathroom, she again started having a hard time catching her breath. I asked a nurse if she could bring a wheelchair because Mommy couldn't walk back to the room. Normally, my mother would have refused the extra help, but not this time. Suddenly she fainted and fell into the wheelchair. My calm exterior turned to sheer panic. I screamed for our dad (even though he wasn't at the hospital yet) and then for Sophie. Steve, Ben, and Sophie came rushing into the hall. Mommy eventually came to, and we later found out that she had pulmonary embolisms—blood clots in both her lungs.

A pulmonary embolism can be life threatening; we're so lucky that Mommy's were caught early. Sometimes it can be too late. For that, we can only thank Mommy's guardian angel, who was undoubtedly watching over her that day. As for Sophie and me, it was really hard to remain calm and not cry. But we knew we had to be strong for her. We couldn't crumble.

Mommy had to stay in the hospital for a week until her blood levels stabilized. So Sophie and I moved into her room that night and never left her side for seven days. Her room had one small couch, and we had to sleep practically on top of each other. Sophie accidentally kicked me in the face during the middle of the night, and we woke up fighting about our sleeping positions. It made Mommy laugh, the way our bickering usually does.

Every day we picked out Mommy's breakfast, lunch, and dinner. We spent our days watching TLC—thank goodness for the *Say Yes to the Dress* and *What Not to Wear* marathons! It cheered Mommy up when she saw the commercials for *DC Cupcakes* because it gave her something fun to talk about with all the nurses who came in. We also gave her mini facials and manicures. We tried to make things as normal as possible for her, so she wouldn't be scared or lonely, but we would secretly cry in the bathroom when no one was around.

Mommy is fine now, and we could not be more thankful. The week we spent in the hospital with her, believe it or not, was one of the most special times in our lives. Even though it was an emotional roller-coaster ride, we were able to fall off the grid for a bit. We didn't answer emails or phone calls; we didn't even go into the bakery. We just focused on getting Mommy healthy. It brought us closer as a family.

Mother's Day is extra special for us now because we appreciate how lucky we are to still have Mommy. She is back to her old self again, still nagging us to have grandchildren and yelling at us for not standing up straight—and we wouldn't want it any other way.

—Katherine

(Left) Mommy, age 7.
(Right) Babee and Mommy at the shore.

Cupcake Flowerpot with Honeybee Yogurt Cupcakes and Buttercream Frosting

This makes a lovely centerpiece for Mother's Day brunch or a sweet alternative to an ordinary bouquet for your mom's special day.

Makes 1 flowerpot with 24 cupcakes

FOR THE CUPCAKES

3 cups sifted all-purpose flour

2 teaspoons baking powder

16 tablespoons unsalted butter

2 cups sugar

5 large eggs

1 cup Greek yogurt

½ cup honey

FOR THE FROSTING

16 tablespoons unsalted butter

4 cups sifted confectioners' sugar

1 teaspoon whole milk

1 teaspoon pure vanilla extract

¼ teaspoon salt

2 teaspoons yellow gel food color

2 teaspoons red gel food color

FOR THE DECORATION

1 terra-cotta flowerpot, about 8 inches wide

1 Styrofoam half-sphere

Chocolate Ganache (page 7)

2 cups Oreo cookie crumbles

thin wooden skewers, 6 to 12 inches long

¼ pound each green, yellow, black, and white fondant

green edible luster dust (optional)

fondant roller

piping gel

edible food marker

white edible luster dust

2 pieces string black licorice

For the cupcakes:

❶ Preheat the oven to 350°F. Line two cupcake pans with twelve paper baking cups each.

2 Sift together the flour and baking powder in a bowl, and set aside.

3 In the bowl of a stand mixer or in a bowl with a handheld electric mixer, cream together the butter and sugar until light and fluffy, approximately 3 to 5 minutes.

4 Add the eggs slowly, one at a time.

5 Add the yogurt, mixing in at low speed.

6 Add the flour mixture slowly, on low speed, stopping to scrape down the bowl when needed. Add the honey. Mix at low speed until just combined.

7 Using a standard-size ice cream scoop, fill each baking cup so that it is two-thirds full, and bake for 16 to 18 minutes or until a toothpick inserted comes out clean. Transfer the pans to a wire rack to cool completely.

For the frosting:

1 In the bowl of a stand mixer or in a bowl with a handheld electric mixer, mix together the butter, sugar, milk, vanilla extract, and salt until light and airy, approximately 3 to 4 minutes.

2 Add the yellow food color, and mix until the color is uniform.

3 Remove the bowl from the mixer stand. Add the red food color and mix it in using an offset spatula, so that there are "streaks" of red in your yellow frosting. Do not overmix, since you want a streaky effect.

4 Using a piping bag fitted with a large star tip, frost each cupcake, following these steps: starting with your piping bag ⅛ inch from the top of the center of the cupcake, swirl the frosting in a circular pattern, going around each circle of frosting until you reach the edge of the cupcake. The frosting should not pile up on top—it should be one large set of rings. This will give your cupcake an abstract "rose" effect.

To assemble the cupcake flowerpot:

1 Start with a terra-cotta flowerpot, and place a hard Styrofoam half-sphere inside. (Foam spheres are available in a variety of sizes at most craft stores.)

2 Drizzle warm Chocolate Ganache onto the foam sphere until it is completely covered, and then sprinkle Oreo cookie crumbles on top of the warm Chocolate Ganache. You now have "soil" in your flowerpot!

3 To attach the cupcakes, insert the wooden skewers into the foam sphere at symmetrical points across the exposed surface. Then place a frosted cupcake onto the exposed end of each wooden skewer so that the sphere is completely concealed by cupcakes.

4 To make the fondant leaves, roll out a sheet of green fondant and cut out leaf shapes. Brush the leaves with the luster dust if you'd like to make them shiny. Rest the leaves on a fondant roller to achieve a curved shape. Once they have hardened (approximately 10 minutes), place the leaves on the frosted cupcakes so that they are scattered throughout the flowerpot.

5 To make the fondant honeybee, pinch a piece of yellow fondant the size of a walnut, and divide it into two pieces in the ratio of one third to two thirds. Roll the larger piece into the shape of an egg (the bee's body) and the smaller piece into a perfect circle (the bee's head). Using piping gel or water, attach the head to the body. Then take thin pieces of black fondant (the thickness of fettuccine) and lay them around the body for its stripes and attach two dots of fondant for its eyes. Roll out a piece of white fondant, and cut out two leaf shapes. Brush them with white luster dust and attach to the bee's back for its wings. Then cut two pieces of string black licorice for its antennae. Stick two tiny black balls of fondant on top for the top of the antennae. Finally, stick the antennae into the bee's fondant head. Place the bee on top of one rose cupcake in the flowerpot.

6 For an extra-special touch, wrap the rim of the flowerpot in an orange, yellow, or red ribbon. Happy Mother's Day!

buttercream sunflowers

If you're getting confident with your piping skills and want to try something a little fancier, try frosting your cupcakes to look like beautiful sunflowers. Just follow the steps below:

1. Using a small round metal tip, pipe a round dab of frosting in the center of your cupcake to anchor your petals.

2. Then, using a U-shaped tip, frost the petals of your flower around the center dab using brisk strokes, pulling up at the end so that the petals hit the edges of your cupcake.

3. Once you have frosted a ring of petals around the center, frost another layer of petals on top of the first layer. Make a third layer of petals a little shorter by shortening your frosting strokes.

4. For a final touch, add a candy center to your flower! ✿

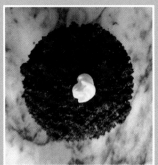

real flowers can be yummy, too

It's always fun to top cupcakes with blooms made from fondant, sugar, or frosting, but real flowers can also be a delicious decoration. Though they can be pricey, the flowers below are completely safe to eat. Just make sure they are from a trustworthy source (not all flowers are safe to eat) and free of pesticides. You can probably find a good assortment in the lettuce and herb section of your local supermarket. Here are some of our favorites:

Basil Flowers A favorite of Greeks. The blossoms are a beautiful white, pink, or purple with a lemon and minty flavor, just like the herb.

Bergamot Citrusy mint flavor. This was one of the sugars we tried for our floral cupcakes from Giuseppe in the "Roller Girls" *DC Cupcakes* episode.

Borage Beautiful blue flowers. We used these to decorate the wedding cupcakes in the "Wedding Recipe" *DC Cupcakes* episode.

Carnations Delicious nutmeg scent. They remind us of Babee, because she grew them in her back-yard flower garden.

Hibiscus Cranberry and lemon flavor. We use hibiscus syrup in our Hibiscus Mango cupcakes.

Impatiens One of Mommy's favorite flowers. They have a sweet flavor.

Lavender Beautiful purple flowers with a floral and citrusy taste.

Lemon Blossoms Citrusy flavor, just like the fruit. We named our Lemon Blossom cupcakes after this flower.

Marigolds Pretty orange and yellow flowers with a spicy taste. They also remind us of Babee.

Mint Flowers Minty flavor, just like the herb.

Orange Blossoms Beautiful blossoms with a citrusy flavor. We named our Orange Blossom cup-cakes after this flower.

Roses Flavors can vary from fruity to spicy. Roses are one of our favorite decorations, since the petals are edible. They taste even better when candied.

Violets Pretty purple and yellow flowers with a sweet flavor. They also taste delicious when candied. ✷

CHAPTER 11

Father's Day

Our Dad at Disney World

Our dad worked full-time when we were kids, so when we did get to spend quality bonding time with him, it was a treat. Like Mommy, our dad's rather spontaneous and thrives on doing things differently. When Mommy would ask him to pick up groceries for the week, instead of going during the day (like most people), he'd hit the twenty-four-hour supermarket at midnight ("There are fewer lines!") and fill up three shopping carts with our favorite snacks. When he'd come home late from work, he'd often walk through the door carrying three large pizzas. We would jump up and down with delight. Our dad loved (and still does!) to act on impulse.

Unlike our aunts and uncles and friends' parents, who planned vacations well in advance, our parents took the fly-by-the-seat-of-the-pants approach to holidays, especially our dad. One Father's Day weekend, he surprised us all: "Why don't we go to Disney World?" We started screaming like crazy! Whose dad does this? Ours! And Mommy, being Mommy, did not object at all—she is always up for anything at any time.

It was a spur-of-the-moment decision and we ran upstairs to our room, packed our small bags, and helped load up the car. Unless there was a body of water in between, we never flew anywhere for vacations; we always drove, no matter how far away it was. Our dad loves to drive. It was Friday afternoon, so our dad figured we'd be in Florida in about twenty-four hours. We stopped in North Carolina to sleep for a few hours, and then continued on. We slept in the car, while our dad drove the entire way. When we finally arrived in Orlando, we checked into the nearest hotel to Disney World that we could find. Our parents weren't ones to make hotel reservations in advance, and this was before the age of the Internet and online booking. Our room had a small kitchen, and we loaded it full with groceries.

Outside were a large pool and barbecue grills. We spent the evening splashing around while our dad grilled burgers. He also took us out for milk shakes later, since he absolutely loved shakes—especially strawberry ones! We got them from a small shacklike roadside restaurant, and they were delicious.

We spent only one day at the Magic Kingdom and Epcot Center and then started the drive back home. Most people would think we were crazy to drive twenty-four hours for just one weekend, but that's how our dad rolled. For us, a big part of the fun of it was the drive itself, playing I Spy in the back seat, singing along to songs on the radio, and going on an adventure together.

Daddy's Strawberry Milk Shakes

This recipe is super simple and a go-to in our household!

Makes 4 tall glasses

2 cups fresh strawberries

2½ cups vanilla ice cream

1 cup whole milk

2 teaspoons pure vanilla extract

seeds from 1 vanilla bean

4 whole fresh strawberries, for garnish

Mix the 2 cups strawberries, ice cream, milk, vanilla extract, and vanilla bean seeds in a blender. Pour into chilled glasses and garnish with whole fresh strawberries. Serve and enjoy!

"Hamburger" Cupcakes

Makes 12 cupcakes

12 yellow cupcakes (page 62)

12 chocolate cupcakes (page 74)

3 cups Vanilla Buttercream Frosting
  (page 136)

2 teaspoons each green, red, and yellow gel
  food color

piping gel

sesame seeds

1 Slice the yellow cupcakes in half, across the middle, so that the top half is your top "bun" and the bottom half is your bottom "bun."

2 Slice the chocolate cupcakes in half, across the middle, so that the top half is your "hamburger patty."

3 Place a chocolate cupcake slice on top of a bottom bun.

4 To make your frosting "mustard," "ketchup," and "lettuce," divide the frosting into three small bowls. To each bowl, add several drops of yellow, red, or green food color, and mix so that you have a yellow-tinted buttercream, a red-tinted buttercream, and a green-tinted buttercream. Place the frostings in three piping bags, each fitted with a narrow round metal tip.

5 To decorate your cupcake hamburger patty, frost a squiggle pattern of yellow buttercream across the surface and around the edge of the chocolate cupcake slice, to create an edge of mustard. Repeat with the red buttercream to create the ketchup and the green buttercream to create the lettuce.

6 Place a top yellow cupcake half on top to form the top bun. Using a pastry brush, lightly brush the top with piping gel or water, and sprinkle sesame seeds on top. Repeat for each cupcake. Serve and enjoy!

CHAPTER 12

Fourth of July

One of our favorite days of the year to be in Washington, DC, is the Fourth of July. There is just something so cool about celebrating the independence of our country in the nation's capital. The national monuments and White House are all lit up, and there are American flags everywhere—on people's lawns and hanging from buildings and cars. Of course, thousands of people descend upon the city, gathering on the grassy lawns along the Potomac River, trying to stake out some prime real estate to watch the awesome fireworks display. We usually try to secure a great spot on the Georgetown waterfront to watch. But it takes some planning!

Usually, because we're so busy at the bakery, we send our parents down early with Poochie to set up the folding chairs and small table. Our dad brings a cooler full of

> *We're grateful to live in a place where you can follow your dreams wherever they take you.*

sodas and water, and Mommy loves to make Italian cold cut sandwiches on thick crusty French baguettes with all kinds of delicious side salads—like coleslaw, pasta salad, and of course her famous potato salad! She always brings a tablecloth and sets up a beautiful arrangement of food.

We come with cupcakes (what else!) and admit we take great pride in noting how many people have our bright pink Georgetown Cupcake boxes at their picnics. Our triple berry cupcakes are red, white, and blue and incredibly delicious—which is why so many people buy them for the Fourth. Sophie creates an American flag made of mini cupcakes that we serve to our friends and family. Patriotically yummy!

We love watching the sun set on the river and feeling the buzz of excitement rush through the crowd as we all anticipate the fireworks. As the sky grows inky black, the fireworks suddenly explode in a glorious kaleidoscope of colors and shapes. We *ooh* and *aah* in unison.

Independence Day is a time for us to reflect and be proud of the country we live in. We're grateful to live in a place where you can follow your dreams wherever they take you.

Recipe for Success

Partying for a Cause

One of the best parts of owning a bakery is the ability to give back to the community and support causes that are important to us. We've found that there are always parties going on benefiting great causes—and what better way to get people to come than to serve cupcakes? They're a great draw for all types of fund-raisers, from happy hours to formal galas. Since we've opened Georgetown Cupcake, we've donated hundreds of thousands of cupcakes to local and national charity events.

One of our favorite ways to give back is through our annual Operation Cupcake, where we send cupcakes to the troops in Afghanistan and other overseas locations for the holidays. Many service people have been away from their families for a long time, and for some it's the first holiday they are spending away from the States, so getting a little treat that reminds them of home means a lot. For the past two years, we've shipped ten thousand cupcakes per year to our troops, and we're going to continue to do it every year.

Be creative with your cupcake causes. Everyone loves a bake sale, but that's just the start. Why not raffle off a cool experience, such as "a dozen cupcakes each month for a year," at a charity auction? Or get together with friends and bake cupcakes to donate to a local soup kitchen around the holidays. A little cupcake can do a lot of good!

American Angel Food Mini Cupcake Flag

This recipe for angel food mini cupcakes topped with fresh whipped cream, blueberries, and raspberries makes the perfect dessert to serve at a Fourth of July party. If you like, you can scale this recipe up to make an even larger flag!

Makes 96 mini cupcakes (or a flag that is 8 minis wide x 12 minis long)

FOR THE CUPCAKES

48 large egg whites

1 teaspoon salt

4 cups sifted all-purpose flour

6 teaspoons cream of tartar

5 cups sugar

4 teaspoons pure vanilla extract

seeds from 4 vanilla beans

FOR THE WHIPPED CREAM

2 pints heavy whipping cream (cold)

½ teaspoon pure vanilla extract

seeds from 1 vanilla bean

½ cup granulated sugar

½ cup sifted confectioners' sugar

FOR THE DECORATION

144 raspberries

96 blueberries

For the cupcakes:

1 Preheat the oven to 350°F, and line four mini cupcake pans with twenty-four paper baking cups each. (If you don't have four pans, you can bake these cupcakes one or two pans at a time.)

2 Pour the egg whites into the bowl of a stand mixer or a bowl with a handheld electric mixer. Add the salt and mix on high speed until stiff peaks form, approximately 2 to 3 minutes.

3 Sift together the flour and the cream of tartar, and add to the mixture on low speed. Add the sugar and the vanilla extract, and mix slowly. Scrape the vanilla bean seeds into the mixture, and mix thoroughly on low speed.

4 Using a mini ice cream scoop, fill baking cups so that they are two-thirds full. Bake for 10 to 12 minutes or until a toothpick inserted comes out clean.

5 Cool on a wire rack for 15 minutes.

For the whipped cream:

In the bowl of a stand mixer with a whisk attachment, or in a bowl with a handheld electric mixer, add all ingredients and whip on high speed for 2 to 3 minutes, until stiff peaks form. Put in piping bag and frost a small round on top of each mini cupcake.

To assemble the "flag":

1 Line up frosted mini cupcakes on a table to create a rectangle that is twelve mini cupcakes wide and eight mini cupcakes high.

2 Starting in the top left corner, place four blueberries on each cupcake, to make a blue square measuring four cupcakes down and six across.

3 Cover each of the remaining cupcakes with two raspberries, side by side in the center of each cupcake, to make red "stripes." Serve and enjoy!

CHAPTER 13

Halloween

As we grew older, when Halloween came around, we wanted our costumes to be more scary *cool* than scary *cute*. While we were both in high school, we decided to throw a Halloween party at home for family and friends, and we determined that we were going to dress up as the Plague—the Black Death! We had just learned about this horrible pandemic in a history class . . . it was gory and gruesome and downright terrifying. How *cool* was that?

At the party, Mommy made her usual white ghost pizzas—pizzas cut in the shape of ghosts, topped with black olive "eyes" and tons of crumbled feta cheese. (As a Greek mom, she always found a way to use all the feta cheese and black kalamata olives that took up most of the space in our fridge!)

We girls were in charge of making our candy bar cupcakes—vanilla and chocolate cupcakes that were loaded up with bits of our favorite Halloween chocolates and candies. We chopped up Kit Kats, M&Ms, Reese's peanut butter cups, candy corn . . . you name it. We mixed in so much candy that the cupcakes came out oversized and gooey (we now know that less is more!).

As the cupcakes cooled on the counter, we went upstairs to our bedroom to get dressed for the party. We wore head-to-toe black—black slacks, boots, and shirts—and were even allowed to put dark eye shadow and eyeliner all around our eyes. Mommy never let us wear a lot of makeup, especially eyeliner and dark eye shadow, so this was definitely a risqué look for us! Sophie came up with the great idea to rub some flour on our faces so that we would look ghostly.

As for our cool costumes, no one could figure out what the heck we were supposed to be. We kept having to explain ("We're the Black Death . . . get it? The Plague?"). Finally we gave up and put on name tags that said "The Plague" so people would stop asking. We made a promise to ourselves that the next year we wouldn't try to be cool. We'd go as something a little easier to recognize . . . like werewolves.

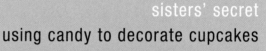

sisters' secret
using candy to decorate cupcakes

Halloween is the perfect time to put all that candy—and your decorating skills—to good use! You can use lots of different types of Halloween candy to decorate your cupcakes for an extra-festive touch. Here are some of our favorite candies and how we use them to jazz up our Halloween cupcakes. ✶

creating spooky fudge spiderwebs

Nothing screams "Halloween" more than creepy cobwebs! Try this easy method for decorating your cupcakes with fudge spiderwebs.

1. Using a squeeze bottle of fudge or Chocolate Ganache (page 7), starting at the top of your cupcake, squeeze a straight line down the middle of your cupcake, touching the bottom.

2. Next, squeeze a straight line going across the middle of your cupcake.

3. Squeeze two lines, cutting each quadrant in half.

4. Finally, connect all the lines with short, slightly curved strokes to finish the web.

5. Repeat for all your cupcakes, serve, and enjoy! ✱

Candy Bar Cupcakes

Makes 24 cupcakes

2½ cups sifted all-purpose flour

2½ teaspoons baking powder

¼ teaspoon salt

8 tablespoons unsalted butter

1¾ cups sugar

2 large eggs

2¼ teaspoons pure vanilla extract

1¼ cups whole milk

2 cups of your favorite Halloween candy, chopped up, plus 24 whole pieces for the topping

FOR THE ORANGE BUTTERCREAM FROSTING

16 tablespoons unsalted butter

4 cups sifted confectioners' sugar

1 teaspoon pure vanilla extract

1 teaspoon whole milk

⅛ teaspoon salt

2 teaspoons orange food color

For the cupcakes:

❶ Preheat the oven to 350°F and line two cupcake pans with twelve paper baking cups each.

❷ Sift together the flour, baking powder, and salt, and set aside.

❸ In the bowl of a stand mixer or in a bowl with a handheld electric mixer, cream together the butter and sugar until light and fluffy, approximately 3 to 5 minutes.

❹ Add the eggs, one at a time, and mix slowly on low speed after each addition.

❺ Add the vanilla extract to the milk, and set aside.

❻ Add one third of the flour mixture to the butter mixture, then gradually add one third of the milk mixture, beating slowly until well incorporated. Add another third of the flour mixture, followed by another third of the milk mixture. Stop to scrape down the bowl as needed. Add the remaining flour mixture, followed by the remaining milk mixture, and beat just until combined.

7 Using a standard-size ice cream scoop, fill each baking cup so that it is two-thirds full.

8 Add 1 tablespoon chopped candy to each baking cup, and mix into the batter with a fork or spoon.

9 Bake for 15 to 18 minutes or until a toothpick inserted into the center of a cupcake comes out clean.

10 Let the cupcakes cool on a wire rack for approximately 20 minutes.

For the frosting:

1 Cream the butter in the mixer on medium speed.

2 Add half of the confectioners' sugar, and mix on low speed. Increase speed to medium once incorporated.

3 Add the vanilla extract to the mixture.

4 Add the remaining confectioners' sugar to the mixture, and mix on medium speed.

5 Add the milk and salt.

6 Once creamed, mix on high speed until smooth.

7 Add the orange food color.

8 Mix on high speed until the color is achieved. Add more food color if you would like a darker orange. Frost each cupcake with a signature swirl (see page xxv), and top with the corresponding Halloween candy. Serve and enjoy!

Tie-Dyed Monster Cupcakes

These playful tie-dyed cupcakes, each adorned with a monster's face made of candy, are perfect for Halloween parties!

Makes 24 cupcakes

FOR THE CUPCAKES

2½ cups sifted all-purpose flour

2½ teaspoons baking powder

¼ teaspoon salt

8 tablespoons unsalted butter

1¾ cups sugar

2 large eggs

2¼ teaspoons pure vanilla extract

1¼ cups whole milk

1 teaspoon each of blue, red, green, and yellow food color

FOR THE VANILLA BUTTERCREAM FROSTING

16 tablespoons unsalted butter

4 cups sifted confectioners' sugar

1 teaspoon pure vanilla extract

1 teaspoon whole milk

⅛ teaspoon salt

FOR THE MONSTER FACES

fondant roller

¼ pound bright blue fondant

3-inch circle cookie cutter

assorted candies

For the cupcakes:

1 Preheat the oven to 350°F, and line two cupcake pans with twelve paper baking cups each.

2 Sift together the flour, baking powder, and salt, and set aside.

3 In the bowl of a stand mixer or in a bowl with a handheld electric mixer, cream together the butter and sugar until light and fluffy, approximately 3 to 5 minutes.

4 Add the eggs, one at a time, mixing slowly on low speed after each addition.

5 Add the vanilla extract to the milk, and set aside.

6 Add one third of the flour mixture to the butter mixture, then gradually add one third of the milk mixture, beating slowly until well incorporated. Add another third of the flour mixture, followed by another third of the milk mixture. Stop to scrape down the bowl as needed. Add the remaining flour mixture, followed by the remaining milk mixture, and beat just until combined.

7 Divide the batter equally into four smaller bowls. To each bowl, add 1 teaspoon of a different food color, and mix with a spoon until the batter is uniformly colored.

8 Then, using a tablespoon, place layers of cupcake batter of different colors in the baking cups. It's okay if your spoonfuls are uneven because this will result in a cool "random" tie-dyed effect. Repeat until all baking cups are two-thirds full.

9 Bake for 15 to 18 minutes or until a toothpick inserted into the center of a cupcake comes out clean.

10 Let the cupcakes cool on a wire rack for approximately 20 minutes.

For the frosting:

1 In the bowl of a stand mixer or in a bowl with a handheld electric mixer, mix the butter, sugar, vanilla extract, milk, and salt until the frosting is light and airy, approximately 3 to 5 minutes.

2 Place the frosting in a piping bag fitted with a large round metal tip. Frost each cupcake with a signature swirl (see page xxv) of Vanilla Buttercream.

To make the monster faces:

1 Roll out a piece of blue fondant, and using a cookie cutter, cut out a circle with a diameter of 3 inches. Place on top of the frosted cupcake to form the monster's face.

2 Using a piping bag fitted with a small round tip, pipe a circle of frosting around the circumference of the blue fondant circle. Pipe two small dots of frosting for the monster's eyes. Pipe another two short linear angled strokes above its eyes to anchor its eyebrows. Pipe one small dot to anchor its nose. Pipe a row of small dots below its nose to represent your monster's teeth.

❸ Next, decorate your monster's face with candy. Line the circle with jellybeans. Cut two short pieces of black licorice, and place them on top of the linear buttercream strokes to form the monster's eyebrows. Place two tiny candy balls on the white dots of frosting to form the pupils of its eyes. Place a German berry candy on top of the dot of white frosting to form its nose. Serve and enjoy!

Mommy's Witch's Brew

This is one of Mommy's creations—a fun, non-alcoholic punch to serve at Halloween parties. If you'd like to make it alcoholic, you can easily substitute champagne, or white or rosé wine, for the grape juice. We recommend serving it with a ladle in a dark cast-iron stockpot, so it looks like a cauldron. Instead of serving it in glasses, try to find dark and spooky mugs or goblets!

Makes 12 servings

4 cups sparkling grape juice

4 cups cranberry juice

4 cups ginger ale

1 pint fresh blueberries

1 pint fresh raspberries

4 large oranges, peeled and sliced into circles

2 cups grapes

Mix all of the ingredients in a large black pot, serve over ice, and enjoy!

CHAPTER 14

Thanksgiving

There is one Thanksgiving that will go down in history in our family. It was the fall of 1997 and the first Thanksgiving after Babee and Papou had passed away. Sophie was coming back from college in New Jersey, and I was still in my final year of high school. Our grandparents had hosted Thanksgiving every year at their house since the day we were born, and it was a holiday that we all looked forward to. This year felt somber because our grandparents were not around and Sophie was gone most of the time, too. Time moved a little slower, and things seemed a little quieter. It was hard to laugh; it was hard to get excited about turkey dinner with all the fixings. But we all put on brave faces and tried our best. Ever since Sophie left for school, I hadn't had anyone to bake with regularly. I missed her. I even missed our fights. We still shared the same room, and

> *Groceries were on the counter, the fridge was wide open, and Mommy was trying to oversee the stove, which had something either bubbling, simmering, or frying on each burner!*

when she got home the day before Thanksgiving, I helped her unload her suitcase. She brought home a cool sweatshirt from Princeton for me. We got into pj's and stayed up all night talking.

The next morning we woke up to the fire alarm going off. It was so loud and jarring that we jumped out of bed. We could hear Mommy yelling out a big "Soweeeee," apologizing for the rude awakening. She was downstairs opening up all the windows to get the smoke out of the house and some fresh air in.

We ran downstairs to find the kitchen in total disarray. Pots and pans were everywhere, groceries were on the counter, the fridge was wide open, and Mommy was trying to oversee the stove, which had something either bubbling, simmering, or frying on each burner! It was total chaos, and no wonder that she had accidentally left one of her oven mitts on a burner, where it burst into flames.

She asked us to run some errands for her and meet up with our cousins. Frankly, I think she just wanted us out of her hair. When we got back home, she told us to get ready for dinner because it was almost ready. We sat with Dad and waited patiently for dinner to be served. But it wasn't ready. Mommy was still in the kitchen, and it was already past 6:00 P.M. She had been in the kitchen for nearly twelve hours!

She looked tired and frazzled and exhausted. When she started to bring out the food, the turkey looked shriveled and dry. She put down a bowl of salad. "Dinner is served!" she announced.

"But where's the rice, potatoes, and vegetables?" Sophie and I asked. What had she been doing for the past twelve hours?

"You will eat what I made!" Mommy yelled. We all sat in silence and shock, looking at the sparse Thanksgiving dinner and afraid to anger Mommy with any more questions.

142   ◉   Katherine Kallinis Berman & Sophie Kallinis LaMontagne

Then Dad asked, "Did you at least make any gravy?" There was silence, and then Mommy turned and gave our dad a dirty look. It was so out of character, we couldn't help ourselves and we all started laughing uncontrollably. It was the first time in a long while that we had laughed, and even Mommy laughed, too. We all couldn't stop laughing. We were so thankful for Mommy's Thanksgiving dinner disaster—it brought joy back into our home.

—*Katherine*

Cranberry Spice "Turkey" Cupcakes with Vanilla Cream Cheese Frosting

Makes 24 cupcakes

1¼ cups sifted all-purpose flour

1½ teaspoons baking powder

¼ teaspoon ground cinnamon

¼ teaspoon ground nutmeg

¼ teaspoon salt

8 tablespoons unsalted butter

1 cup sugar

2 large eggs

¼ cup water

1 cup fresh or frozen cranberries

Vanilla Cream Cheese Frosting (page 154, without the rum)

¼ pound each brown, white, black, and orange fondant

fondant roller

piping gel

144 pieces of candy corn

For the cupcakes:

❶ Preheat the oven to 350°F, and line two cupcake pans with twelve paper baking cups each. Sift together the flour, baking powder, cinnamon, nutmeg, and salt in a bowl, and set aside.

❷ In the bowl of a stand mixer or in a bowl with a handheld electric mixer, cream together the butter and sugar until light and fluffy, approximately 3 to 5 minutes.

❸ Add each egg slowly, one at a time, mixing after each addition.

❹ Add one third of the flour mixture to the butter mixture, followed by one third of the water. Mix slowly. Then add another third of the flour mixture, followed by another third of the water. Mix slowly again. Finally, add the last third of the flour mixture and the last third of the water. Mix until all the ingredients are incorporated.

5 Scrape down the bowl, and add the cranberries. Fold in using a spatula until the cranberries are scattered throughout the batter.

6 Using a standard-size ice cream scoop, fill each baking cup so that it is two-thirds full. Bake for 18 to 20 minutes or until a toothpick inserted comes out clean.

7 Let the cupcakes cool and then frost with Georgetown Cupcake's signature swirl (see page xxv).

To make the fondant turkeys:

1 Roll out a small ball of brown fondant, approximately the size of a golf ball, to form the body of your turkey. Then roll out a ball of brown fondant, approximately half the size of the first ball, to form the head of your turkey. Attach the head to the body using piping gel or water.

2 Roll out two small balls of white fondant, each approximately the size of a pea, to form the eyeballs of your turkey.

3 Roll out two small balls of black fondant, each approximately the size of half a pea, to form the pupils of your turkey's eyes. Using piping gel or water, attach the pupils to the eyeballs, and the eyeballs to the turkey's head.

4 Roll out a small piece of orange fondant, and shape it into a crescent to form the turkey's beak. Attach it to the turkey's head using piping gel or water.

5 Roll out four small pieces of brown fondant and shape them into rounded tear-drops to form feathers.

6 Let the fondant turkey and feathers set for 5 to 10 minutes, and then place the turkey on top of a cupcake, with the feathers placed behind.

7 Line up six pieces of candy corn, pointed side down on the brown fondant feathers behind the turkey's body to form another layer of feathers.

Kolokithopita (Greek Pumpkin Phyllo Pastries) Because

we grew up in a Greek household, phyllo dough was always a staple in our kitchen. Babee used to make her own from scratch, spending hours and hours rolling her dough with a rolling pin to get it very thin. Now you can buy great phyllo dough at the supermarket, and it's one of the rare instances where we think it's okay to use a frozen dough. Babee often filled her phyllo pastry with feta cheese or spinach, or walnuts and cinnamon, but pumpkin was one of our favorites, and she typically made it in the fall. This recipe is a perfect sweet and savory appetizer for your Thanksgiving feast.

Makes about 36 triangles (depending on size)

3 pounds baked and pureed pumpkin (fresh or canned)

1 cup honey

½ cup sugar

3 teaspoons ground cinnamon

1 teaspoon ground nutmeg

20 sheets phyllo dough

1 cup unsalted butter, melted

❶ Preheat the oven to 350°F. Grease a baking sheet with butter.

❷ Mix together pumpkin, honey, sugar, cinnamon, and nutmeg in a medium bowl.

❸ Cut phyllo dough into vertical strips about 2 inches wide, and cover the pile of phyllo strips with a clean, damp tea towel.

❹ Lay one phyllo strip flat on a workspace in front of you. Using a pastry brush, brush the surface of the phyllo dough with an even coat of melted butter. Place a tablespoon of the pumpkin filling at the end of the phyllo strip. Starting at the end with the pumpkin filling, fold the phyllo dough over as you would a flag until the phyllo is the shape of a triangle. Place on baking sheet.

❺ Repeat until all of the pumpkin filling is used up.

❻ Bake for 30 minutes or until the tops of the triangles are golden brown.

setting a table

Setting a table is one of those things that you learn how to do once, and always seem to forget when you are actually doing it. Here's a fun photo showing what goes where at each place setting. When Thanksgiving rolls around and you blank out, just turn to this page. We've got you covered! ✳

Bread knife and plate

Dessert fork

Dessert spoon

Place card

Water goblet

Red wine glass

White wine glass

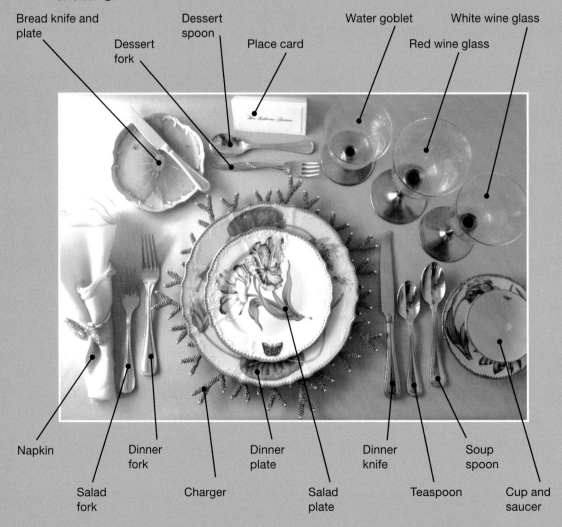

Napkin

Salad fork

Dinner fork

Charger

Dinner plate

Salad plate

Dinner knife

Teaspoon

Soup spoon

Cup and saucer

Recipe for Success

Set a Timeline and Work Backward!

~~~~~~

Thanksgiving is one of those holidays when so many things need to be done, it can feel overwhelming. The best way to prevent a holiday meltdown? Make a timeline and work backward. Start at the time your guests will be sitting down at the table, and work back from there. This will help keep you on track throughout the day and will prevent the day from getting out of control. Here's an example of a timeline we did for a recent Thanksgiving, which included cooking a fifteen-pound turkey:

6:00 P.M.   Everyone sits down at the table.

5:55 P.M.   Carved turkey placed on the table.

5:50 P.M.   All food except turkey placed on the table.

5:45 P.M.   Carve the turkey.

5:30 P.M.   Plate all the side dishes.

5:15 P.M.   Take the turkey out of the oven.

4:00 P.M.   Make all the side dishes.

3:30 P.M.   Make the salad and salad dressing.

2:00 P.M.   Make the cupcakes.

1:15 P.M.   Set the table.

1:00 P.M.   Put the turkey in the oven.

12:30 P.M. Prep the turkey.

12:00 P.M. Prep all ingredients and get all tools and utensils ready.

CHAPTER ⊚ 15

Christmas

A Holly Jolly Christmas

When Christmas 2000 rolled around, I was in my first job, and Katherine was a junior in college. She and I were sharing an apartment in Arlington, Virginia, and were getting ready to drive home for the holidays. There was a certain anticipation to "going home" for the holidays, now that we lived so far away. The weeks before Christmas were busy as always, packed with work and with everyone rushing to get things done before the holidays.

Finally it was the day before Christmas Eve, around 5:00 P.M., and we were free! We both got back to the apartment that day and flopped down on the couch. Then we realized that we were going home the next day and couldn't arrive empty-handed. Neither of us had done any Christmas shopping whatsoever. The thought of going to

151

> *Staying up all night baking for our family gave us an adrenaline rush.*

the jam-packed mall made us uneasy. So we did what felt natural to us: we decided to bake. We got into our old Jeep and drove to the supermarket. Through the aisles we went with our shopping cart, zipping along to the Christmas music playing in the background. We quickly loaded up on everything—flour, sugar, cinnamon, nutmeg, cloves, ginger, confectioners' sugar, sanding sugar, and then eggs, milk, butter, and vanilla! On display were the cutest Christmas mugs, on sale because it was so close to Christmas. So we loaded up on several sets of those as well. On the way back to our place, we made a quick stop for Chinese takeout, since we needed fuel for our all-night baking marathon.

When we got to the apartment, it was already around 7:00 P.M., and we quickly unloaded our baking supplies. We changed into comfy T-shirts and Christmas sweatpants and turned on the Christmas music, preheated the oven, got out our pans, and embarked on our baking adventure. The hours passed quickly, and trays of gingerbread men, almond cookies, and chocolate peppermint cupcakes made their way out of the oven, quickly taking up all of our kitchen counter space. Before we knew it, it was 2:00 A.M., and we were only halfway through our baking. We made some hazelnut coffee for ourselves and pressed on—mixing more batter, the smell of nutmeg and cloves all around us.

Several sisterly blowouts later (about who was working harder and who was slacking and who forgot to add the baking powder), we were almost done. We had baked so many rounds of goodies that melted butter had started to accumulate on the bottom of the oven. Around 4:00 A.M. we saw several flashes of light. The butter was catching fire, and we literally were seeing fireballs! That was it. We turned off the oven and stopped baking for the night before we burned the whole place down.

We iced our cookies, frosted our cupcakes, and finished around 5:00 A.M. We looked around the kitchen to see what a mess we had created. We had to be on the road at 8:00 A.M. to make it home in time for dinner and church that night. Now, as the sun started to rise, we were getting a little sleepy, but we quickly plated all of our homemade sweets, wrapping them with cellophane and red, green, and gold plaid silk ribbon. For some relatives, we created gift baskets with cupcakes, gingerbread men, a canister of our favorite hot cocoa, and the fun Christmas mugs. For others, we created a basket with a set of four Christmas-themed dessert plates with our chocolate peppermint cupcakes on top, again tying them with cellophane and beautiful ribbon. We carefully tied on homemade gift tags and lined everything up on the dining table.

We washed the dishes, took a quick catnap, and woke up to our alarm clock at 7:00 A.M. We hopped into the shower, got dressed, and loaded up the car—the Jeep was filled to the roof with delicious-smelling sweet treats. As we drove on the snowy interstate on Christmas Eve, the snowflakes falling all around us, we weren't tired at all. Staying up all night baking for our family gave us an adrenaline rush. We were energized and couldn't wait to get home to share our wonderful Christmas gifts with our family!

—*Sophie*

Christmas Ornament Chocolate Eggnog Cupcakes with Rum Cream Cheese Frosting

Makes 18 cupcakes

FOR THE CUPCAKES

1¼ cups sifted all-purpose flour

½ teaspoon baking soda

¼ teaspoon salt

8 tablespoons unsalted butter

1¼ cups sugar

2 large eggs

1¼ teaspoons pure vanilla extract

1 cup eggnog

½ cup dark rum, or rum extract for a
    non-alcoholic version

½ cup sifted cocoa powder

FOR THE CREAM CHEESE FROSTING

4 tablespoons unsalted butter

4 cups sifted confectioners' sugar

¼ teaspoon pure vanilla extract

6 ounces cream cheese

¼ cup dark rum, or rum extract for a
    non-alcoholic version

FOR THE DECORATION

¼ pound each red, green, and gold fondant

fondant roller

¼ cup edible luster dust (gold, silver, and/or white)

¼ cup each cupcake toppings of your choice,
    such as nonpareils or candy balls

For the cupcakes:

1 Preheat the oven to 350°F. Line a cupcake pan with twelve paper baking cups, and a second pan with six baking cups.

2 Sift together the flour, baking soda, and salt in a bowl, and set aside.

3 In the bowl of a stand mixer or in a bowl with a handheld electric mixer, cream together the butter and sugar on medium speed until light and fluffy, approximately 3 to 5 minutes.

4 Add the eggs one at a time, mixing slowly after each addition.

5 Combine the vanilla and eggnog in a large liquid measuring cup.

6 Add one third of the flour mixture to the butter mixture, then gradually add one third of the eggnog mixture, beating slowly until well incorporated. Add another third of the flour mixture, followed by another third of the eggnog mixture. Stop to scrape down the bowl as needed. Add the remaining flour mixture, followed by the remaining eggnog mixture, and beat just until combined.

7 Add the rum (or rum extract), and mix until just combined.

8 Add the cocoa powder, beating on low speed just until incorporated.

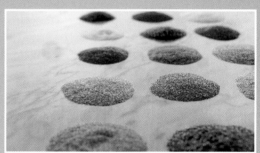

9 Using a standard-size ice cream scoop, fill each baking cup so that it is two-thirds full. Bake for 18 to 20 minutes (start checking at 15 minutes) or until a toothpick inserted into the center of a cupcake comes out clean. Transfer the pans to a wire rack to cool completely.

For the frosting:

In the bowl of a stand mixer or in a bowl with a handheld electric mixer, mix all the ingredients for approximately 3 to 5 minutes, until the frosting is light and airy. Frost each cupcake with a thick layer of the frosting using an offset spatula.

To decorate the cupcakes as "ornaments":

Roll out flat pieces of fondant in a variety of colors, about ¼ inch thick. Cut out eighteen circles with a diameter of 3 inches, enough to cover each cupcake with one circle. Brush the surface of each circle with gold, silver, or white luster dust, or a combination of all three. Next, press your favorite cupcake toppings into each circle to create festive patterns (see the photo on page 150). Place a circle on each cupcake. Then wrap each cupcake in tissue paper, and place it in a square box, wrapped with ribbon, to serve. Happy Christmas!

Georgetown Cupcake Chocolate Peppermint Bark

This is a delicious treat to whip up around the holidays. It makes the perfect addition to any dessert spread as well as a lovely parting gift for guests.

Makes 2 pounds bark

2 cups dark or semisweet chocolate chips

1 to 2 teaspoons pure peppermint extract
  (add more to taste)

2 cups white chocolate chips

1 cup crushed peppermint candy or candy
  canes

1 Fill a small saucepan half full with water and bring to a gentle boil. Place a glass bowl on top of the pan so that it sits snugly on top. Add the dark or semisweet chocolate chips, and melt slowly, stirring constantly. Add the peppermint extract and mix thoroughly.

2 Line a small (8 × 4-inch) rectangular baking dish with parchment paper. Pour dark chocolate into the baking dish, and place it in the refrigerator for 20 to 30 minutes to chill and harden.

3 While the dark chocolate is chilling, melt the white chocolate chips in another glass bowl using the same technique. When the white chocolate is completely melted, pour it on top of the chilled and hardened dark chocolate.

4 Sprinkle the crushed peppermint on top so that it completely covers the white chocolate. Place it in the refrigerator for 20 to 30 minutes to chill and harden.

5 Remove from the refrigerator and turn upside down to remove the hardened peppermint bark. Break the bark into small- or medium-size pieces.

crushing the perfect peppermint

We love crushed peppermint around Christmastime, but sometimes it can be tricky to crush to exactly the right size. If you don't crush it enough, it can look like giant "teeth" on your cupcakes, and if you crush it too much, it can be too powdery. We obsessed for a year looking for the perfectly sized precrushed peppermint. Here are some easy tips to achieve that perfect look at home:

• Place your candy canes or peppermint candies in a zip-lock bag.

• Pound the bag with a rubber mallet or the bottom of a measuring cup. Keep pounding the bag until you get pieces of peppermint roughly the size of peas.

• Pour the contents of your bag over a strainer, and strain all the excess "powder" into a bowl.

• You'll be left with perfect pieces of crushed peppermint!

CHAPTER 16

Hanukkah

Traditions Old and New

Hanukkah is a spiritual and special holiday that I recently started to celebrate. My husband is Jewish, and I converted to Judaism before we were married. It's a beautiful religion and culture, and it has many of the same fundamental principles of Greek Orthodoxy that I live my life by: loving-kindness to others, charity, family, and thankfulness. For me, it was a natural fit.

Over the years, Ben would tell me stories about his family's Hanukkah celebrations when he was growing up. The whole family would get together—uncles, aunts, cousins, and family friends—and spin the dreidel. The Bermans would nosh on crisp potato latkes (pancakes) topped with applesauce and sour cream before they handed out small gifts to each loved one. They would also light the menorah, a beautiful can-

> *The glow of the candles lit up the room and warmed our spirits.*

delabra that holds nine candles, one for each of the eight nights of Hanukkah and the *shamash* in the middle to light them.

I was fascinated and surprised by how Hanukkah and Christmas have the same heart. They are both about family coming together to celebrate over food and being thankful for all the blessings in life. After hearing Ben recount his childhood memories, I was very excited to celebrate my first Hanukkah. I loved the idea that we were starting a new tradition together and that we would one day be passing these rituals on to our children.

My new aunt Nina and uncle Jimmy bought us a beautiful silver and glass menorah from Israel. The menorah is not just a pretty centerpiece; it has religious significance as well. I learned that a long time ago in ancient Israel, the Jews needed to keep a sacred lamp lit inside the temple. During a period of conflict, only one container of oil remained, enough to light the lamp for only a day. But miraculously, the small amount of oil was able to keep the lamp burning for eight full days and nights! This is why Hanukkah is also known as the festival of lights and why it is eight days long.

On a chilly December night in 2011, I took out our menorah and placed it on a table by the window. I also got out the silk challah cover and prayer shawls that our rabbi had given us during my conversion. I was so excited to celebrate with all of our new Judaica! We invited friends and family who were staying in Washington, DC, for the holidays. We had a huge turkey dinner that Sophie helped me prepare. It was also *my* family's first Hanukkah, and they had a wonderful time celebrating a new tradition from a new culture.

Everyone was silent as I carefully placed one candle in the menorah to represent the first night, and a second candle as the *shamash*. The glow of the candles lit up the room and warmed our spirits. Everyone gathered in close, shoulder to shoulder, arm in arm, as we said a prayer over the lighting of the candles.

Then it was time to party! Ben began singing all of these wonderful songs about Hanukkah and taught us the words and melodies: "Oh dreidel, dreidel, dreidel . . . I made it out of clay! And when it's dry and ready, my dreidel I will play!" and "Hanukkah, oh Hanukkah, come light the menorah, let's have a party, we'll all dance the hora!"

Then it was time for the gifts! Ben and I had decided that we wanted to give each other something to commemorate the holiday—but nothing too extravagant. I ripped open my box to find all sorts of wonderful bath soaps. Ben opened his wrapped package from me and pulled out a ski hat and gloves to keep him warm during the winter. He loves that blue wool hat and wears it all the time!

After we exchanged gifts, I told everyone I had a special surprise—my personal twist on the Hanukkah holiday. Ben smiled; he knew cupcakes were going to be part of his Hanukkahs from now on! Blue and white are the colors of the Israeli flag, and they have long been associated with Jewish culture. So I decided to make Blue Velvet cupcakes with a light and fluffy cream cheese frosting. To top it all off, I rolled out some blue fondant and added a Star of David on top of each cupcake. I brought them out on a platter decorated with gold foil–wrapped coins known as *gelt,* and everyone dove in. They'll now be a permanent fixture on our menu at Georgetown Cupcake during the winter season so that everyone can take part in the magical holiday that is Hanukkah.

—*Katherine*

Star of David Blue Velvet Cupcakes

Makes 12 cupcakes

3¼ cups sifted all-purpose flour

1 teaspoon salt

12 tablespoons unsalted butter

1¾ cups sugar

2 large eggs

4 tablespoons blue food color

1 teaspoon pure vanilla extract

2½ tablespoons sifted cocoa powder

1½ cups whole milk

1½ teaspoons baking soda

1½ teaspoons apple cider vinegar

vanilla cream cheese frosting (page 154, without the rum)

¼ pound dark blue fondant

fondant roller

Star of David cookie cutter

For the cupcakes:

1 Preheat the oven to 350°F. Line a cupcake pan with twelve paper baking cups.

2 Sift together the flour and salt in a bowl, and set aside.

3 In the bowl of a stand mixer or in a bowl with a handheld electric mixer, cream together the butter and sugar until light and fluffy, approximately 3 to 5 minutes.

4 Add the eggs one at a time, mixing slowly after each addition.

5 Using a whisk, beat together the blue food color, vanilla, and cocoa powder. Add to the mixer bowl and mix until incorporated.

6 Add one third of the flour mixture to the butter mixture, followed by one third of the milk, and mix slowly until incorporated. Add another third of the flour mixture, followed by another third of the milk, and mix slowly until incorporated. Add the final third of the flour mixture, followed by the final third of the milk, and mix on low speed until incorporated.

7 In a small bowl, add the baking soda to the apple cider vinegar. Add the fizzing mixture to the batter, and mix until just incorporated.

8 Using a standard-size ice cream scoop, fill each baking cup so that it is two-thirds full. Bake for 16 to 18 minutes. Transfer the pan to a cooling rack to cool completely.

9 Frost each cupcake with a signature swirl (see page xxv) of vanilla cream cheese frosting.

To make the fondant Stars of David:

Roll out the fondant. Using the cookie cutter, cut out twelve blue stars. Let harden and place a single star on top of each cupcake.

GEORGETOWN CUPCAKE

cupcakes

$2.75 each | $15 half dozen | $29 dozen
single cupcake box $.50 | gift wrap $1.50

today's cupcakes

carrot	vanilla & chocolate
chocolate ganache	milk chocolate birthday
chocolate & vanilla	vanilla²
chocolate birthday	chocolate²
vanilla birthday	red velvet
chocolate coconut	gluten-free lava fudge

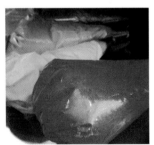

Part 3

EVERYDAY PARTIES

*From Sunday brunch to tea with friends,
every day is an opportunity to turn ordinary
occasions into sweet memories!*

CHAPTER 17

Sleepovers

Our First Sleepover

When our cousins used to come over to play, we always begged our parents for a sleepover. But no matter how much we pleaded, there was always some reason we couldn't do it—school the next day, church the next day, a math test to study for. Then finally, during the first day of our spring break in 1988, they said yes! Our three cousins, Mary, Elizabeth, and Annie, were allowed to come for a sleepover. We couldn't wait. We were nine and eleven at the time, and our cousins were the same ages. Did we stay up all night? Oh, yes!

We all wore our matching pink and purple pajamas that our aunt Irene bought for us for Christmas every year. We built a huge fortress of sheets in our family room using the couches as tent anchors. Then we set up our sleeping areas. The oldest cousins, Sophie and Mary, were on one side, and the youngest, Katherine, Elizabeth, and Annie, were on the other side. We played Nintendo for hours and hours. Katherine was the best and most talented video gamer in our family; no one could beat her scores on Super Mario Brothers, so we would let her take the controllers and nervously cheer her on.

Mommy, being the super-cool mom that she was, brought us a never-ending stream of snacks. At 11:00 P.M., she carried in a pepperoni pizza and homemade garlic bread. By midnight we were ready for something sweet, so we baked up a batch of cupcakes and ate them right out of the oven, along with the cotton candy that our cousins brought over. We loved the way it melted on our tongues. At 2:00 A.M., we got the munchies again, so Mommy whipped up some of her famous caramel- and chocolate-covered popcorn. She never served microwave popcorn. She, like Babee, would make it the old-fashioned way, on the stove. She would use her big cast-iron pot, pour a little oil in the bottom, and sprinkle in the kernels. With her oven mitts on, she would shake, shake, shake the pot to get those kernels popping! Then she would lightly salt the popcorn and drizzle melted caramel and chocolate on top. It was the perfect salty-sweet late-night snack.

We built a huge fortress of sheets in our family room using the couches as tent anchors.

We talked all night long and called our local radio station, K-LITE FM, to play our favorite New Kids on the Block songs. We painted our nails in cool shades of pink, and practiced doing different hairstyles and makeup on one another. If one of us started to nod off and fall asleep, the rest of us would wake her up!

Around 3:00 A.M., Mommy came in to check in on us. She saw that we still weren't asleep, so she made us snuggle up in our sleeping bags as she told us her famous bedtime story of "Maria." We think this is based on some well-known fairy tale, but Mommy definitely put her own spin on it. It started with Maria falling into a well and being transported to a fantasyland where she needs to find her way back home. Along the way, she has to shake some apples from a tree, bake some bread in an oven . . . the story goes on and on (and looking back on it now, we're not even sure it had a moral or point to it!). It took Mommy nearly two hours to tell. We're not even sure how it ends because no one ever lasts till the "She lived happily ever after" part.

So somewhere close to 5:00 A.M., just as the sun was rising, Mommy finished telling the story of Maria, and we were all sound asleep.

sisters' secret

storing buttercream frosting

It's always best to make your buttercream fresh, right before you plan to use it. If you plan on making it in advance, however, you can store it at room temperature overnight or in the refrigerator for two or three days. If you store it in the refrigerator, let it warm up to room temperature before using by placing it on the counter for 2 to 3 hours or popping it in the microwave for 30 seconds at a time, until it is soft. Before you use it, whip it up in your mixer again to get it back to being light and airy.

Cotton Candy Cupcakes Topped with Cotton Candy–Stuffed Fondant Pillows

Makes 24 cupcakes

FOR THE CUPCAKES

2½ cups sifted all-purpose flour

2½ teaspoons baking powder

¼ teaspoon salt

8 tablespoons unsalted butter

1¾ cups sugar

2 large eggs

2¼ teaspoons pure vanilla extract

1¼ cups whole milk

1 cup pink cotton candy, broken up into small quarter-size "puffs"

FOR THE PINK BUTTERCREAM FROSTING

16 tablespoons unsalted butter

4 cups sifted confectioners' sugar

1 teaspoon pure vanilla extract

1 teaspoon whole milk

⅛ teaspoon salt

½ teaspoon red food color

1 cup clear sanding sugar

FOR THE DECORATION

¼ pound purple fondant

fondant roller

white edible luster dust

patterned fondant stamps

pastry cutter with a ruffled edge

piping gel

1 cup pink cotton candy

For the cupcakes:

❶ Preheat the oven to 350°F, and line two cupcake pans with twelve paper baking cups each.

❷ Sift together the flour, baking powder, and salt, and set aside.

❸ In the bowl of a stand mixer or in a bowl with a handheld electric mixer, cream together the butter and sugar until light and fluffy, approximately 3 to 5 minutes.

4 Add the eggs one at a time, mixing slowly on low speed after each addition.

5 Add the vanilla extract to the milk, and set aside.

6 Add one third of the flour mixture to the butter mixture, then gradually add one third of the milk mixture, beating slowly until well incorporated. Add another third of the flour mixture, followed by another third of the milk mixture. Stop to scrape down the bowl as needed. Add the remaining flour mixture, followed by the remaining milk mixture, and beat just until combined.

7 Use a spatula to scrape down the sides of the mixing bowl. Fold in the cotton candy pieces using the spatula, so that your batter becomes streaked with pink sugar.

8 Using a standard-size ice cream scoop, fill each baking cup so that it is two-thirds full. Bake for 15 to 18 minutes or until a toothpick inserted into the center of a cupcake comes out clean.

9 Let the cupcakes cool on a wire rack for approximately 20 minutes.

For the frosting:

1 Add the butter, sugar, vanilla extract, milk, salt, and red food color to the bowl of a mixer, and mix until light and airy, approximately 3 to 5 minutes.

2 Place the frosting in a large piping bag fitted with a plain round metal tip, and frost each cupcake with a signature swirl (see page xxv) of Pink Buttercream. Then cover the entire surface of the cupcakes with the sanding sugar.

To make the fondant pillows:

Roll out the purple fondant approximately ⅛ inch thick. Brush with some white luster dust. Using the pastry cutter with the ruffled edge, cut out two small rectangles, 3 inches long by 2 inches wide, for each pillow. With a pastry brush or your fingertip, moisten the edges of one of the rectangles with piping gel or water. Place a small pinch of cotton candy on top of the center of the fondant rectangle, being careful not to touch the piping gel or water. Then place the other rectangle on top, sealing the cotton candy in the "pillow" by pressing along the edges. Place a stuffed pillow on top of each cupcake. Serve at your slumber party and enjoy!

Mommy's Caramel- and Chocolate-Drizzled Popcorn

Mommy loves to pop popcorn the old-fashioned way, in a pot on the stove, but you can also use your air popper or a plain microwave kind!

Makes 10 cups

10 cups popped plain popcorn

¼ cup melted butter

2 teaspoons salt

1 cup melted white chocolate

1 cup melted milk chocolate

1 cup caramel (page 74)

Pour the popcorn into a large pot or bowl. Drizzle with the butter and salt, and toss so that the butter evenly coats the popcorn. Then drizzle popcorn with the white chocolate, milk chocolate, and caramel, and toss so that the drizzle is equally distributed over all the popcorn. Serve in individual bowls and enjoy!

CHAPTER 18

Tea Parties

Our First Tea

Tea parties are the height of entertaining: elegant, sophisticated, and royal. In Canada, where we grew up, teatime was a big deal. The country has many British traditions, and tea is definitely one of them. As little girls, we would have a casual after-school "tea-time" with Babee and Papou every afternoon at their house. But the first time Babee ever took us to a *real* tea, it was to the fancy Eaton's department store restaurant, when we were four and five years old.

At Eaton's, tea was served at 4:00 P.M. sharp. We sat with our grandmother at an elegant table covered with a white linen tablecloth, beautiful white bone china teacups and plates, and a scrumptious array of sandwiches and sweets on silver platters. Babee dressed us up for the occasion—we wore matching pink and blue dresses and little

white gloves, and each of us carried a small purse. As we bit into our cucumber sandwiches and looked at all the ladies around us, we couldn't help but feel so "grown up." Babee let us have only a small sip of tea, which she loaded up with honey, but it didn't matter. We felt like real ladies who lunch just the same.

After our first real "tea" at Eaton's, we were inspired to have a tea party at home. One lazy afternoon, when our parents were at work and Babee was napping in the living room, we snuck upstairs and draped a bath-towel "tablecloth" over an upside-down laundry basket we used for our tea table. We borrowed Babee's fine china teacups and teapots, filling them with milk, juice, and water. Then we pulled a few red roses from the veranda rosebushes and put them in a small glass vase.

We sat cross-legged on the floor and served our special guests—our Cabbage Patch dolls, Georgeanne and Lena, and Katherine's favorite stuffed lion, Roary. Our topics of discussion were wide-ranging, but mostly centered around our favorite cartoons and toys. In our imaginations, we thought of ourselves as well-dressed women with white gloves and fancy hats, sitting at antique tables with ornate linens, daintily sipping gourmet tea and nibbling finger sandwiches with friends

> *Then we had a "surprise visitor," our dog Carmen, who also took a sip out of Babee's china with his big pink tongue.*

while discussing fashion or current events. Then we had a "surprise visitor," our dog Carmen, who also took a sip out of Babee's china with his big pink tongue!

We sat there for hours, and then, as we heard Babee stirring downstairs, we quickly started to clean up. But she was too fast and caught us! Instead of yelling at us or reprimanding us for taking out her good china (and letting Carmen drink out of it!), she smiled and laughed and asked us why we hadn't invited her. So our make-believe tea party became a little ritual, with Babee (and Carmen!) as a regular guest.

Although we didn't *exactly* re-create the tea parties that we saw in the movies or in the lounges of fancy hotels, it was our chance to practice the art of entertaining in grand style. Now, as adults, going to tea is one of our favorite pleasures. There is something very civilized and peaceful about sitting down to a formal tea. Though we're so busy, we try to make it an annual tradition and take Mommy to tea!

sisters' secret

vintage teacups as serving pieces

We absolutely adore Babee's vintage Queen Anne teacups, and even though we don't have a full set, we love to use them for entertaining. One of the best things about vintage teacups is that they look even better when they are mixed and matched with different patterns and styles. The best places to find unique vintage teacups are garage sales and flea markets, where you can get them at great prices and build your collection. For tea parties, we love to remove our cupcakes from their wrappers, place them inside our teacups on saucers, and serve them to our guests just like that! ✪

Blackberry Cupcakes with Lemon Filling

The great thing about these cupcakes is that (in addition to being super yummy) the filling can be prepared the night before and stored in the refrigerator.

Makes 24 cupcakes

FOR THE LEMON FILLING

¼ cup sugar

2 large egg yolks

¼ cup sifted all-purpose flour

¼ cup cornstarch

1 cup whole milk

2 tablespoons heavy cream

2 tablespoons freshly squeezed lemon juice

2 tablespoons grated lemon zest

FOR THE CUPCAKES

2½ cups sifted all-purpose flour

2½ teaspoons baking powder

¼ teaspoon salt

8 tablespoons unsalted butter

1¾ cups sugar

2 large eggs

2¼ teaspoons pure vanilla extract

1¼ cups whole milk

seeds from 1 vanilla bean

1 cup fresh blackberries, diced

FOR THE FROSTING

16 tablespoons unsalted butter

4 cups sifted confectioners' sugar

1 teaspoon whole milk

1 teaspoon pure vanilla extract

¼ teaspoon salt

lemon zest

½ cup diced blackberries, plus 24 whole fresh blackberries, for garnish

For the filling:

❶ In the bowl of an electric mixer with a paddle attachment, mix the sugar and the egg yolks for 4 to 5 minutes.

❷ In another large bowl, sift together the flour and the cornstarch.

3 Add the flour and cornstarch to the egg mixture slowly, mixing on low speed for 1 to 2 minutes or until smooth.

4 In a medium saucepan, heat the milk on medium heat, just until it starts to boil.

5 Switch your mixer to the whisk attachment, then add the *hot* milk slowly to the mixer and whisk continuously at medium speed while pouring the milk, to keep the mixture smooth and without lumps or curdles.

6 Add the heavy cream, lemon juice, and lemon zest, and mix thoroughly for 2 to 3 minutes.

7 Pour the mixture back into the saucepan, and cook over medium heat until it boils. *Note: The mixture must be hand-whisked constantly during this time.* After it reaches boiling, whisk for 2 more minutes, until it thickens.

8 Remove from heat. Let the mixture come to room temperature before pouring it into a bowl. Refrigerate for at least 2 hours to chill. Then place in a plastic squeeze bottle to use.

For the cupcakes:

1 Preheat the oven to 350°F. Line two cupcake pans with twelve paper baking cups each.

2 Sift together the flour, baking powder, and salt in a bowl, and set aside.

3 In the bowl of a stand mixer or in a bowl with a handheld electric mixer, cream together the butter and sugar until light and fluffy, approximately 3 to 5 minutes.

4 Add the eggs one at a time, mixing slowly after each addition.

5 Combine the vanilla extract and the milk in a large liquid measuring cup. Carefully scrape the vanilla bean seeds into the milk.

6 Add one third of the flour mixture to the butter mixture, then gradually add one third of the milk mixture, beating slowly until well incorporated. Add another third of the flour mixture, followed by another third of the milk mixture. Stop to scrape down the bowl as needed. Add the remaining flour mixture, followed by the remaining milk mixture, and beat just until combined.

7 Using a spatula, gently fold in the blackberries.

8 Scoop batter into baking cups so that each is two-thirds full, and bake for 15 to 18 minutes or until a toothpick inserted into the center of a cupcake comes out clean. Transfer the pans to a wire rack to cool completely.

For the frosting:

1 Place all of the ingredients in the bowl of a mixer, and beat until frosting is light and airy, approximately 3 to 5 minutes.

2 Using an apple corer, twist and remove the center of the cupcakes and discard. Make sure to press all the way to the bottom until you reach the paper wrapper, so that you can fill it with as much filling as possible. Then squeeze the filling to completely fill the hole in the center of each cupcake.

3 Using a piping bag fitted with a large round metal tip, frost each cupcake with a signature swirl (see page xxv) of Blackberry Frosting, and garnish with lemon zest and a fresh blackberry on top. Serve in vintage teacups and enjoy!

Cucumber and Cream Cheese Tea Sandwiches

Makes 4 sandwiches

8 slices white bread

4 ounces low-fat cream cheese

1 large cucumber

salt and pepper to taste

½ teaspoon chopped fresh dill

½ teaspoon cayenne pepper

olive oil to taste

large flower-shaped cookie cutter

1 Toast the bread.

2 Using a butter knife, spread a thin layer of cream cheese on each slice of toast.

3 Peel the cucumber, and using a utility knife, cut it into ⅛-inch slices. In a bowl, mix the cucumber with the salt, pepper, dill, cayenne pepper, and a touch of olive oil.

4 Place four cucumber slices on each piece of toast. Place the remaining pieces of toast on each, to make a total of four sandwiches.

5 Using the cookie cutter, press down into each sandwich in order to cut out a flower-shaped finger sandwich.

sisters' secret
using your cupcake tools for savory treats!

Cookie cutters are not just for desserts! You can use these cutters to shape your sandwiches into hearts and flowers, or to cut "windows" in the bread to give a peek at the filling inside. ✖

White Cheddar and Marmalade Tea Sandwiches

Makes 4 sandwiches

8 slices white bread

4 ounces white cheddar cheese

4 ounces marmalade or preserves of your choice

large heart-shaped cookie cutter

orange zest, freshly grated

1 Toast the bread.

2 Using a cheese peeler, peel the cheese into eight to twelve thin slices, approximately 1/16 inch thick.

3 Place two or three slices of cheese on each of four slices of the toast.

4 Using a butter knife, spread a thin layer of marmalade or preserves on the other four slices of toast.

5 Press one of the slices of toast with the marmalade on top of one of the slices with the cheese. Repeat three times to make a total of four sandwiches.

6 Using the cookie cutter, press down into each sandwich in order to cut out a heart-shaped finger sandwich.

7 Garnish each sandwich with a dash of orange zest and serve!

CHAPTER 19

Brunches

A Lazy Summer Brunch

During the summer before opening Georgetown Cupcake, we knew that once we opened for business, our lives were going to become crazy. So we decided to take one last mini vacation and visit our dad's family in Greece in the summer of 2007. We flew to Athens with Mommy, our dad, Steve, and Ben, excited to be back in our family's homeland after five years.

We all crammed into a tiny rental car to make the long drive through the mountains to our dad's village, Meliti. Rental cars in Europe are really small, and Mommy had packed several large suitcases full of gifts for the family, so there was practically no room! Katherine and I had to sit in each other's laps for the entire drive. To make matters worse, our dad couldn't remember how to drive a car with a manual transmission, so we would travel fifty feet, then stall, then restart the car, over and over. But eventually he got the hang of it, and we were on our way.

> It was a simple brunch, but everything was fresh and crisp and just plucked off the tree.

The drive up to the village was beautiful, first following along the coast of the Aegean Sea outside of Athens and then turning inland, past Mount Olympus and up through the mountains. We drove through many of Greece's small, rural villages and often passed flocks of sheep and shepherds along the way. The roads were steep and there were no streetlights, so we had to take it slow and steady, stopping occasionally at a roadside stand for a fresh sandwich.

After driving through the night, we arrived at our first stop, our uncle's house outside of one of the larger cities in northeastern Greece. The house was on a farm where he grew fresh peaches, figs, and other fruits. As we pulled up to the door, our uncle, aunt, and cousins were all waiting on the front steps with open arms. It was midmorning and we were tired from driving all night, but they had set up a table in the yard with a beautiful brunch feast: peaches, figs, and apples that had been picked straight from the trees on the farm, scrambled eggs from the small chicken house in the backyard, and freshly squeezed orange and grapefruit juices.

There were bowls of oranges and grapefruits on the table along with an old-fashioned juicer that our cousin was dutifully operating. Katherine bit into a fresh peach, and it was so juicy that it squirted Mommy right in the eye! Mommy started to get upset but then saw a basket of fresh figs . . . one of her weaknesses . . . and grabbed a handful to enjoy. Our aunt prepared hot *loukoumades,* which are Greek fritters dipped in honey and cinnamon. There were also pitchers of hot Greek coffee and iced tea, with fresh peach slices dancing in the pitcher.

It was a simple brunch, but everything was fresh and crisp and just plucked off the tree. We all sat around the table for hours. In the village, the first meal of the day is often brunch, late in the morning, and people take their time and enjoy it. Lunch is not usually until 4:00 P.M. or so, and then dinner is around 10:00 P.M. or sometimes even later. One thing we love about our Greek relatives is their ability to slow down and savor the mornings. The first meal of the day isn't a rushed frenzy of coffee and cereal as you frantically race out the door. It's all about relaxing, indulging in the tastes and aromas surrounding you, and enjoying the company.

Katherine, our grandmother Baba Domna (our dad's mother), Sophie, and Steve.

The Greek countryside.

Ginger Peach Cupcakes

Makes 24 cupcakes

2½ cups sifted all-purpose flour

2½ teaspoons baking powder

½ teaspoon ground ginger

¼ teaspoon salt

8 tablespoons unsalted butter

1¾ cups sugar

2 large eggs

2¼ teaspoons pure vanilla extract

1¼ cups whole milk

1 cup fresh peaches, diced

FOR THE FROSTING

16 tablespoons unsalted butter

4 cups sifted confectioners' sugar

1 teaspoon whole milk

1 teaspoon pure vanilla extract

¼ teaspoon salt

½ teaspoon ground ginger

FOR THE DECORATION

¼ pound each light orange, brown, and green
   fondant

piping gel

white sanding sugar

1 small fruit crate

For the cupcakes:

1 Preheat the oven to 350°F. Line two cupcake pans with twelve paper baking cups each.

2 Sift together the flour, baking powder, ginger, and salt in a bowl, and set aside.

3 In the bowl of a stand mixer or in a bowl with a handheld electric mixer, cream together the butter and sugar until light and fluffy, approximately 3 to 5 minutes.

4 Add the eggs one at a time, mixing slowly after each addition.

5 Combine the vanilla extract and milk in a large liquid measuring cup.

6 Add one third of the flour mixture to the butter mixture, then gradually add one third of the milk mixture, beating slowly until well incorporated. Add another third of the flour mixture, followed by another third of the milk mixture. Stop to scrape down the bowl as needed. Add the remaining flour mixture, followed by the remaining milk mixture, and beat just until combined.

7 Using a spatula, gently fold in the peaches.

8 Scoop batter into baking cups so that each is two-thirds full, and bake for 15 to 18 minutes or until a toothpick inserted into the center of a cupcake comes out clean. Transfer the pans to a wire rack to cool completely.

For the frosting:

1 Place all of the ingredients in the bowl of a stand mixer or in a bowl with a hand-held electric mixer. Beat until the frosting is light and airy, approximately 3 to 5 minutes.

2 With a piping bag fitted with a plain round metal tip, frost each cupcake with a signature swirl (see page xxv) of frosting.

To make the fondant peaches:

Roll a piece of light orange fondant the size of a large gumball into a round sphere. Using your thumb, press a long crease from the top to bottom of one side of the peach to create an indentation. Using a pastry brush, brush the peach with piping gel or water, and then dip it into a small bowl of white sanding sugar. Cut out a small leaf of green fondant and a small stem of brown fondant, and attach to the top of your peach using piping gel or water. Place on top of a cupcake, and repeat. Serve cupcakes in a roadside stand–style fruit crate, such as from a farmers' market.

Greek Cinnamon Cupcake, Honey, and Yogurt Parfaits

We like to use glass dessert dishes that are at least 4 inches tall so there's plenty of room to display these lovely parfaits.

Makes 24 parfaits

FOR THE SYRUP

2 cups sugar

2 cups water

peel of 1 orange, sliced into long strips

peel of 1 lemon, sliced into long strips

FOR THE CUPCAKES

2 cups sifted all-purpose flour

3 teaspoons baking powder

1 teaspoon ground cinnamon

½ teaspoon ground cloves

8 tablespoons unsalted butter

¾ cup sugar

5 large eggs

½ cup whole milk

1 teaspoon freshly grated orange zest

FOR THE PARFAITS

6 cups Greek yogurt

3 cups honey

3 cups crushed walnuts

Cinnamon Buttercream Frosting (page 270)

ground cinnamon for dusting

For the syrup:

Combine the sugar, water, and orange and lemon peel in a small saucepan, and boil for 5 to 6 minutes. Strain into a bowl, separating out the orange and lemon peel, and set aside until cool.

For the cupcakes:

❶ Preheat the oven to 350°F, and line two cupcake pans with twelve paper baking cups each.

❷ Sift together the flour, baking powder, cinnamon, and cloves in a bowl, and set aside.

3 In the bowl of a stand mixer or in a bowl with a handheld electric mixer, cream together the butter and sugar until light and fluffy, approximately 3 to 5 minutes.

4 Add the eggs one at a time, mixing slowly after each addition.

5 Add one third of the flour mixture to the butter mixture, followed by one third of the milk, and mix slowly. Follow with another third of the flour mixture, followed by another third of the milk, and mix. Add the final third of the flour mixture, followed by the final third of the milk, and mix until just combined. Stop as needed to scrape down the sides of the bowl.

6 Add the orange zest, and mix until just combined.

7 Using a standard-size ice cream scoop, fill each baking cup so that it is two-thirds full, and bake for 18 to 20 minutes or until a toothpick inserted comes out clean.

8 When the cupcakes have cooled, pierce the tops with a fork to create small holes and channels. Then pour the cooled syrup over the cupcakes, allowing it to seep in through the holes.

To assemble the parfaits:

Have your tall glass dessert dishes ready, and remove the cupcakes from their wrappers. Place a cupcake at the bottom of each dish. To each dish, add 4 heaping tablespoons Greek yogurt, followed by a drizzle of 2 tablespoons honey and 1 to 2 tablespoons crushed walnuts. Top with a signature swirl (see page xxv) of Cinnamon Buttercream Frosting and garnish with a dusting of ground cinnamon. Serve and enjoy!

Peach Nectar Iced Tea

Makes 8 cups

6 cups water

4 large fresh peaches

10 packets black tea

8 cups ice cubes

sugar or sugar substitute, to taste

24 fresh mint leaves

❶ In a large pot, boil the water.

❷ Slice the peaches into eighths.

❸ Place the packets of black tea (we prefer Earl Grey) in the boiling water, along with half of the peach slices, and remove from heat. Allow to steep for 10 minutes.

❹ Place a strainer over the top of a large glass pitcher. After the tea has steeped, pour the tea mixture through the strainer into the pitcher.

❺ Add the ice cubes to the pitcher, stirring slowly.

❻ Add the remaining peach slices to the pitcher.

❼ Sweeten the tea to taste. Serve with fresh mint leaves, and enjoy!

Greek Loukoumades (Greek Fritters) These sweet mini pastries
are made of deep-fried dough soaked in sugar syrup, honey, and cinnamon.

Makes 36 to 48 loukoumades (depending on size)

1 package dry yeast

2 cups warm water

1½ teaspoons sugar

4½ cups sifted all-purpose flour

1 teaspoon salt

8 cups vegetable oil, for frying

2 cups honey

¼ cup ground cinnamon

❶ In a large bowl, dissolve the yeast in 1 cup of the water and the sugar.

❷ Add 2 cups of the flour to the yeast mixture, and beat with a whisk until smooth.

❸ Cover the bowl and place in a warm oven (150°F) to rise for 30 minutes, or until the batter has doubled in size.

❹ When the batter has doubled, add the remaining water and flour, and the salt. Cover and return to the oven (at 150°F) to rise for approximately 1 to 2 hours, or until the surface of the dough begins to bubble.

❺ In a large metal pot, heat vegetable oil (enough to fill your pot one-quarter full) to hot.

❻ Drop 1 tablespoon of dough at a time into the oil, until the pot is full of dough balls, or loukoumades. (You can probably fit ten in a large pot.)

❼ Turn down the heat and fry over low-medium heat until the loukoumades become puffy and golden brown.

❽ Remove them using a large slotted spoon, and place them in a bowl lined with a paper towel.

9 Once you have all the loukoumades in the bowl, remove the paper towel. Pour the honey all over the loukoumades and sprinkle them with the cinnamon.

10 Using a large spoon, toss the loukoumades so that they are completely covered with honey and cinnamon. Serve while hot, and enjoy!

Recipe for Success

Working Vacations

It's hard to get away when you run a bakery that's 24/7. On our last trip to Greece during the summer of 2007, the summer before we opened Georgetown Cupcake, we found ourselves desperately trying to find an Internet café so that we could email our future landlord about our lease. Even though we hadn't yet started our business, it was our first "working vacation." Now we're pretty much tied to Georgetown Cupcake every single day. We love every moment, but there are times when you do have to get away, like *your honeymoon!* Believe it or not, however, I managed to sneak in some work then as well. I went to Tahiti and visited a vanilla bean farm. Tahiti is where

some of the world's best vanilla is made, and it is one of the few places in the world where these beans are harvested. The vanilla beans are picked and then left out to dry in the hot sun. They are massaged daily by hand to work out the moisture in them, which is what gives them their beautiful aroma and taste.

After weeks of lying in the sun and getting massaged (not a bad life!), the vanilla beans are measured and bundled together. They are then packaged and shipped all over the world. I left the farm with a kilogram of Tahitian vanilla beans.

It's important to have fun on your travels, but remember that work doesn't always have to be boring and dull. Working during your vacation doesn't have to be a bad thing—you might discover and learn something new about what you do, and come home even more excited to get back to the grind!

—*Katherine*

CHAPTER 20

Dinner Parties

A Marathon Dinner Party

Since we opened Georgetown Cupcake, hosting a dinner party has become logistically very complicated. By the time the shop closes, it's usually well past dinnertime, and all we want to do is go home and rest after being on our feet all day. But on one summer Sunday in 2008, friends of ours were coming into town, and we wanted to welcome them with an extra-special dinner.

Since it was a Sunday and we were closing at 7:00 P.M., we put together what we thought was a well-oiled plan that would have everyone seated at the dinner table, ready for the first course, by 8:30 P.M. The night before, we went to the grocery store and picked up all of the ingredients that we needed. We stayed up late into the night doing as much preparatory work as possible: Katherine chopped fresh onions, mushrooms, and peppers while I cut chicken breasts into strips and marinated them in a combination of olive oil, lemon juice, salt, pepper, and oregano. I also baked a batch of our Blueberry Cheesecake Cupcakes, which had a delicious graham cracker crust. I placed them in the refrigerator since, unlike all of our other cupcakes, these are best served after being refrigerated overnight. Finally, we set out our dinnerware, utensils, wineglasses, and napkins on the counter along with bowls for snacks.

The plan was straightforward: We would close the shop promptly at 7:00 P.M., race home, and have the table set and snacks (a cheeseboard with artisanal cheeses, honey, cranberry chutney, and rustic bread as well as stuffed peppers) on the coffee table by 7:45. Our friends would arrive at 8:00 P.M., which would leave a half hour for wine, conversation, and snacks before sitting down for dinner. Following a fresh mesclun salad, our main course would be grilled chicken mixed with pasta and roasted vegetables.

Well, the best-laid plans often go awry . . . especially when the hosts are in the cupcake business! The shop was extremely busy that day, and we did not serve the final customer until after 7:30 P.M. I called Steve and told him to start grilling the chicken while we frantically closed up the shop. As we were driving home, Steve called with the next crisis: we did not have a lighter for the grill! We stopped at a convenience store, picked one up, and made it home by 8:00. The grill was cold, nothing was on the table, and we were frazzled and breathless, not to mention covered in flour and frosting from the bakery.

Of course, the doorbell rang!

We raced around, trying to get things back on track, but then finally gave up. So what if the peppers didn't come out with the other appetizers? Who cared if the main course wasn't served till 9:30? We were all having a wonderful time, just letting the dinner party unfold naturally. It was a great lesson for us: we could let go, improvise, relax, and "go with the flow." A good hostess makes plans; a great hostess is flexible enough to change them!

—*Sophie*

quick and easy table centerpieces

In a rush? Here are some quick ideas for chic centerpieces you can put together in no time for an elegant-looking table!

- Bowl of fresh seasonal fruit

- Bowl of fresh seasonal vegetables

- Monochrome flowers in a glass cube vase

- Cake stand with cheese, crackers, and honey drizzle

- Cake stand with dessert: Cupcakes make the best dinner centerpieces, even for super-fancy dinner parties! Here's one we made for an ultra-fancy dinner in honor of former president Bill Clinton! ✯

Blueberry Cheesecake Cupcakes with Blueberry Compote

Makes 12 cupcakes

FOR THE CRUSTS

1 cup graham cracker crumbs

1½ tablespoons sugar

½ tablespoon unsalted butter, melted

FOR THE CUPCAKES

½ pound softened cream cheese

¼ pound mascarpone cheese

⅔ cup sugar

2 large eggs

1 teaspoon fresh lemon juice

½ teaspoon pure vanilla extract

1 teaspoon freshly grated lemon zest

1 cup fresh or frozen blueberries

FOR THE COMPOTE TOPPING

4 pints blueberries

1 cup sugar

4 teaspoons fresh lemon juice

confectioners' sugar, for dusting

For the crusts:

Preheat the oven to 350°F. Line a cupcake pan with twelve paper baking cups. Mix together the crumbs, sugar, and melted butter, and press 2 tablespoons of the mixture into each baking cup. Bake for 12 minutes at 350°F, then take out of the oven.

For the cupcakes:

❶ Whip together the cream cheese and mascarpone cheese. Add the sugar, and beat until light and fluffy, approximately 3 to 5 minutes.

❷ Add the eggs one at a time, mixing slowly after each addition.

❸ Add the lemon juice, vanilla, and lemon zest, and mix.

❹ Using a spatula, gently fold in the blueberries.

5 Using a standard-size ice cream scoop, fill each baking cup so that it is two-thirds full, and bake for 20 minutes. Let cool and place in the refrigerator for at least 2 hours before serving.

For the topping:

Place blueberries, sugar, and lemon juice in a small saucepan, and warm on medium-high heat until the sugar is completely dissolved and the blueberries start to bubble and break apart. Let cool at room temperature. Place one tablespoon of compote on top of each cupcake, and dust with a small amount of confectioners' sugar. Serve on a fancy cake stand and enjoy!

Part 4

OUTDOOR GET-TOGETHERS

Celebrate the great outdoors with sweet treats for friends and family!

CHAPTER 21

Campouts

A Night Under the Stars

It was a hazy summer's night, and we were tweens camping . . . in the backyard! A few hours before the sun set, we rifled through the garage and dug out a big blue tarp, a tent, and our sleeping bags. Then we found the perfect spot in the backyard to set up camp. No matter how many times we tried, it was a big production to set up the tent. After a few tries, we gave up and hung the tarp overhead on poles. Even if it wasn't perfect, it still did the job.

We didn't just rely on the sleeping bags to keep us warm. Our dad helped us set up a little fire pit away from the tent. We carefully lit a fire so we could warm our feet and roast s'mores. Like almost everything we do, we had different opinions about the best technique for making the perfect marshmallow-chocolate-graham-cracker sandwich.

Sophie held the marshmallow about six inches above the flame, turning it slowly and trying to get it golden brown on all sides. I, on the other hand, liked my marshmallows crispier on the outside and more gooey in the center. So I held the marshmallow in the flame until it caught fire, then pulled it out and blew out the flame to achieve my perfect s'more.

When we were ready to go into the tent, Mommy came out with a hose, turned on the water, and put out the fire.

"Are you sure you want to spend the night outside?" she asked, raising an eyebrow. She didn't think we could handle it.

This made us even more determined to prove to her that we could rough it. "We're sure!" we replied. We bundled up in our flannel pajamas and puffer jackets and tried to close our eyes and fall asleep. The cool night air blew through the trees and sent goose bumps up our arms. An owl hooted off in the distance. We were in familiar surround-

Sophie and Katherine playing in the backyard, July 1983.

ings, but the darkness and the shadows made everything look and feel different. Our imaginations got the best of us.

"What's that noise?" I asked. We heard some rustling in the bushes (probably from a raccoon).

"It's a bear!" we screamed hysterically, running into the house. Mommy, of course, was waiting up for us on the couch, grinning from ear to ear. Thankfully, she didn't say, "Told you so!"

We hugged her tight, happy to be safe and sound.   —*Katherine*

sisters' secret
working with marshmallow and other gooey fillings

When working with marshmallow topping, it is important to work quickly! When melted over a double boiler, marshmallow topping takes on the properties of a liquid and is easy to use. Once you remove it from the heat, however, it starts to congeal immediately. Scoop your marshmallow topping into a plastic squeeze bottle right away, and use an extra-wide nozzle to fill your cupcakes. If the marshmallow starts to congeal in the bottle, do *not* reheat inside the microwave; the marshmallow will expand and then explode over the rim of the bottle! Instead, place the bottle in a hot-water bath for a few minutes. When you are done, squirt any remaining topping into a small glass bowl. After a few minutes, you will have a solid marshmallow to enjoy! ✪

Toasted Marshmallow Campfire Cupcakes

Sophie demonstrated this recipe in the "Firehouse" episode of *DC Cupcakes*. Since the frosting is a traditional pure marshmallow frosting, it is critical to work quickly before the marshmallow seizes up and you have one giant marshmallow stuck in your piping bag!

Makes 18 cupcakes

FOR THE GRAHAM CRACKER BOTTOMS

1½ cups graham cracker crumbs

2½ tablespoons sugar

1 tablespoon unsalted butter, melted

FOR THE CUPCAKES

1¼ cups sifted all-purpose flour

½ teaspoon baking soda

¼ teaspoon salt

8 tablespoons unsalted butter

1¼ cups sugar

2 large eggs

1¼ teaspoons pure vanilla extract

1 cup whole milk

½ cup sifted cocoa powder

2 cups warm Chocolate Ganache (page 7)

FOR THE MARSHMALLOW FROSTING

1⅔ cups cold water

5 tablespoons unflavored gelatin

1¼ cups cold water

5 cups sugar

digital thermometer

5 teaspoons pure vanilla extract

kitchen blowtorch

For the graham cracker bottoms:

Preheat the oven to 350°F. Line a cupcake pan with twelve paper baking cups and a second pan with six baking cups. Mix together the crumbs, sugar, and melted butter, and press 2 tablespoons of the mixture into each baking cup. Bake for 12 minutes at 350°F, then take out of the oven.

For the cupcakes:

1 Sift together the flour, baking soda, and salt in a bowl, and set aside.

2 In the bowl of a stand mixer or in a bowl with a handheld electric mixer, cream together the butter and sugar until light and fluffy, approximately 3 to 5 minutes.

3 Add the eggs one at a time, mixing slowly after each addition.

4 Combine the vanilla extract and milk in a large liquid measuring cup.

5 Add one third of the flour mixture to the butter mixture, then gradually add one third of the milk mixture, beating slowly until well incorporated. Add another third of the flour mixture, followed by another third of the milk mixture. Stop to scrape down the bowl as needed. Add the remaining flour mixture, followed by the remaining milk mixture, and beat just until combined.

6 Add the cocoa powder, beating on low speed just until incorporated.

7 Using a standard-size ice cream scoop, fill each baking cup so that it is two-thirds full. Bake for 18 to 20 minutes (start checking at 15 minutes) or until a toothpick inserted into the center of a cupcake comes out clean. Transfer the pan to a wire rack to cool completely.

8 Once cupcakes are cool, using an apple corer, remove the centers. Then put Chocolate Ganache in a squeeze bottle, and fill the centers of the cupcakes with hot fudge so that they are overflowing. Set aside until you're ready to frost.

For the frosting:

1 Switch your mixer to the whisk attachment.

2 In the mixer bowl, pour the 1⅔ cups cold water. Sprinkle the gelatin over the water. Let sit for approximately 2 minutes.

❸ In a small saucepan, warm the 1¼ cups water and the sugar on medium-high heat. Stir until the sugar is dissolved. Then boil the mixture until the temperature reads *exactly* 238°F on a digital thermometer. This is the "candy soft ball" stage. Remove immediately from heat.

❹ Add the boiling syrup to the mixer bowl containing the water and gelatin. Whisk on low speed for 5 minutes until mixture cools. Add the vanilla extract. Then whisk on high speed until the mixture is white, soft, fluffy, and glossy—about 10 minutes.

❺ *Immediately* put the frosting into a piping bag and frost the chocolate cupcakes. The Marshmallow Frosting will harden fast.

❻ With a kitchen blowtorch, torch the top and sides of the frosted cupcakes until they are golden brown. Serve on a platter and enjoy!

making your own cupcake picks

If you're not inclined or don't have the time to make custom fondant decorations for your cupcakes, you can still jazz them up by decorating them with "cupcake picks." They are easy to make on a home computer and printer. Simply print out your design on thick card stock and cut out each design using scissors. Or you could use a craft paper punch to give them an extra-special touch. Next, tape a toothpick or a cocktail pick to the back of your design punch-out, and place the toothpick on top of the cupcake. Voilà! ✪

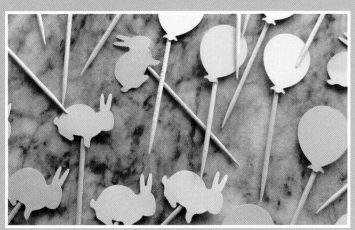

CHAPTER ◉ 22

Pool Parties

Lounging by the Pool

For kids everywhere, nothing is more exciting than a pool party on a hot summer day. Even though we did not have a pool of our own growing up, we absolutely loved swimming, and our parents enrolled us in swimming lessons almost as soon as we were able to walk. We breezed through the lessons and quickly made it to the advanced levels.... We must have been fish in a prior life!

One hot day in July, when Sophie had just turned eight years old, our parents decided to take us to a local pool at a park right on the shore of Lake Ontario. But this was no ordinary pool . . . it was a wave pool, where you could pretend that you were swimming in the Hawaiian Pacific, with its legendary waves for surfing! When we told our cousins that we were going to the wave pool, they naturally wanted to come too, so we made a family day of it.

The park had charcoal grills, so Mommy packed a cooler full of hot dogs, corn on the cob, and potato salad, and our aunt and uncles packed all sorts of snacks, including chips and homemade cookies. When we got to the park, our dad went off to light the grill, and we sprinted straight to the wave pool and dove in. The waves were really strong, and we tried to stand up in the water as if we were riding the waves like professional surfers. When our dad came to tell us that lunch was ready, we didn't want to get out of the pool. Only one thing could lure us away from the waves . . . icy treats! Right next to the pool was an ice cream stand where you could buy old-fashioned sundaes, ice cream sandwiches, and brightly colored popsicles. Sophie had a scoop of vanilla ice cream with butterscotch and hot fudge sauce, while I had two ice cream sandwiches, all before having lunch!

We didn't realize it at the time, but these summer days at the pool would be a source of inspiration for our approach to summer entertaining at Georgetown Cupcake. We developed summer flavors with fresh citrus fruit, and one of our favorite things to eat are our Lemon Blossom, Orange Blossom, and Key Lime cupcakes, frozen! It's like having a pool party every day at our shop.

—*Katherine*

Citrus Orange or Lime Icy Cupcake Pops

Makes 36 cupcake pops

FOR THE CUPCAKES

2½ cups sifted all-purpose flour

2½ teaspoons baking powder

¼ teaspoon salt

8 tablespoons unsalted butter

1¾ cups sugar

2 large eggs

2¼ teaspoons pure vanilla extract

1¼ cups whole milk

½ cup freshly squeezed orange or
lime juice

FOR THE ORANGE OR LIME
BUTTERCREAM FROSTING

16 tablespoons unsalted butter

4 cups sifted confectioners' sugar

1 teaspoon pure vanilla extract

1 teaspoon whole milk

⅛ teaspoon salt

½ cup freshly grated orange or lime zest

FOR SERVING

lollipop sticks

5 cups white chocolate chips, melted in a
glass bowl

½ cup freshly grated orange or lime zest

For the cupcakes:

❶ Preheat the oven to 350°F, and grease a cupcake pan with butter or line with twelve paper baking cups.

❷ Sift together the flour, baking powder, and salt in a bowl, and set aside.

❸ In the bowl of a stand mixer or in a bowl with a handheld electric mixer, cream together the butter and sugar until light and fluffy, approximately 3 to 5 minutes.

❹ Add the eggs, one at a time, and mix slowly after each addition.

5 Add the vanilla extract to the milk in a liquid measuring cup.

6 Add one third of the flour mixture and one third of the milk mixture to the butter mixture, and mix slowly until incorporated. Add another third of the flour mixture and another third of the milk mixture, and mix until fully incorporated. Add the final third of the flour mixture and the final third of the milk mixture, and mix on low speed until fully incorporated. Stop to scrape down the side of the bowl as needed.

7 Add orange or lime juice, depending on which flavor you're making, and mix thoroughly on low speed.

8 Using a standard-size ice cream scoop, fill each well of the cupcake pan so that it is two-thirds full, and bake for 16 to 18 minutes or until a toothpick inserted comes out clean.

9 Cool the cupcakes on a wire rack.

For the frosting:

Combine all the ingredients in the bowl of a stand mixer or in a bowl with a handheld electric mixer. Beat until frosting is light and fluffy, approximately 3 to 5 minutes.

To assemble the cupcake pops:

1 Line a baking sheet with parchment paper.

2 Crumble the cupcakes into a large bowl by rubbing them together.

3 Add the frosting to the bowl and mix gently with a spatula. When the crumble becomes incorporated into the frosting, the cake balls are ready to be formed.

4 Wash your hands thoroughly or put on disposable food-safe gloves, as you will be using your hands to form the cake balls.

5 Roll some of the cake mixture in your hands to create a ball around the size of a golf ball, and place on parchment paper. Repeat until all the cake mixture is used. You should have approximately thirty-six balls.

6 Dip a tip of a lollipop stick in the melted white chocolate.

7 Insert the chocolate-dipped end of the lollipop stick into a cake ball. Repeat until all cupcake pops are formed, and reserve the remaining white chocolate.

8 Put the cupcake pops in the freezer to harden for 1 hour.

9 Remove the cupcake pops from the freezer, and dip them into the melted white chocolate.

10 Hold the cupcake pops over the bowl of white chocolate until the excess chocolate drips away.

11 Lightly sprinkle orange or lime zest on each cupcake pop. Put back in the freezer for 1 hour.

12 Serve frozen and enjoy!

Ice Cream Cone Cupcakes

Makes 24 ice cream cone cupcakes

24 ice cream cones (your favorite type)

chocolate cupcake batter (page 74)

Vanilla Buttercream Frosting
   (page 136)

ice cream toppings of your choice, such as hot
   fudge, rainbow sprinkles, crushed toffee,
   hazelnuts, or caramel

24 maraschino cherries

1 Preheat the oven to 350°F, and wrap foil over the top of a cake pan that is at least 3 inches deep.

2 Pierce holes in the foil, and place the ice cream cones standing up in the holes.

3 Using a mini ice cream scoop, transfer the cupcake batter into the ice cream cones.

4 Bake the cupcakes for 18 to 20 minutes or until a toothpick inserted comes out clean. Transfer the pan to a wire rack to cool completely.

5 Using Georgetown Cupcake's signature swirl (see page xxv), frost the top of each cupcake with Vanilla Buttercream Frosting.

6 Garnish with your favorite ice cream toppings.

7 Add a cherry on top, serve, and enjoy!

> ### sisters' secret
> ### keeping ice cream cones and cupcake pops upright
>
> If you're serving the cupcake pops and ice cream cone cupcakes in this chapter as part of a dessert buffet or as a table centerpiece and they won't be eaten right away, one of the quickest and least expensive ways to display them is to stick them into glass containers filled with brightly colored jelly beans or other color-coordinated candies. And here's the best part—you can also eat the display! ✪

Katherine's Old-Fashioned Coke Floats

Sometimes the best things in life are the simplest. We made these old-fashioned Coke floats almost every weekend in the summer when our cousins came over to visit. They still bring back great memories of when we were kids, and they are the perfect sweet drink to pour at any outdoor gathering. Serve with cute striped straws in retro glasses for an extra-special touch.

Makes 4 tall glasses

8 scoops vanilla ice cream, or your favorite
   flavor
4 cans Coca-Cola (or cherry Coke or other
   soda)

❶ Put two scoops of ice cream in a tall glass. (Try using a really good vanilla bean ice cream, like Tahitian vanilla.)

❷ Pour Coca-Cola over the ice cream in the glass. Throw in a decorative straw and watch the drink fizzle. Make three more, serve, and enjoy!

Beach Parties

A Weekend in Paradise

This was a once-in-a-lifetime baking gig! We were asked to bake for a celebrity wedding (hint: the couple met on the set of his music video!) on Necker Island, a private island owned by Sir Richard Branson, in the middle of the Caribbean. We were on cloud nine!

Then reality set in. We were told that there were no baking utensils and very few ingredients on the island. So we would have to ship all our staples, like Madagascar Bourbon vanilla extract and King Arthur flour, and equipment—pans, sifters, whisks, graters, bowls, scoops, and more—in two large suitcases. If we were missing *anything,* we would be out of luck for days!

There were no direct flights to the island, so we had to take three different planes and a boat to get there. The flight from Washington, DC, to Puerto Rico was bumpy, but that was nothing compared to the flight on the tiny plane from Puerto Rico to the island of Tortola! We bounced in the sky like a toy plane darting in and out of clouds over the beautiful blue waters. Once we landed, we had to jump onto a speedboat that would take us to the island of Virgin Gorda. The boat ride was so rocky that we almost fell out a couple of times. We both hunkered down, choosing to sit on the bottom of the boat in case we hit another wave. Once we got to Virgin Gorda, our hair was a total mess from the windy seas, but we went straight to work. We had one day to find all our ingredients and bake the coconut cupcakes for the rehearsal dinner and a tropical key lime wedding cake for the big day.

Sourcing coconuts and limes was not difficult at all— they were the freshest and best the island had to offer.

Sourcing coconuts and limes was not difficult at all— they were the freshest and best the island had to offer! Milk, on the other hand, was nearly impossible to find. In fact, we were told that there was no fresh milk on the island and that the residents used only powdered milk! We had never used powdered milk in any of our recipes—what the heck were we going to do? The humidity was also a problem. It was blazing hot and humid, and there was no air-conditioning.

The humidity in the kitchen was our worst enemy. Each time we tried to sift the flour and confectioners' sugar, it would just clump back up again! But the real shock came when we were told that we were allowed to have access to the kitchen only from midnight to 6:00 A.M. to make the wedding cake. Basically, we would be baking it in the middle of the night!

One of us creamed the butter and sugar in the large mixer, adding the wet and dry ingredients, while the other zested the pile of limes and scraped the vanilla beans. We worked throughout the night, trying to stay cool in our pink tank tops as the old ovens heated up in the more than 100-degree weather. A large iguana and a couple of turtles came to the door to visit. It was one of the most challenging environments we had ever baked in, but also the most beautiful: outside the kitchen door we could see the moon reflected in the calm ocean waves.

We didn't sleep that night. Instead, we took the layers of the key lime cake to the one room on the island that did have air-conditioning. The florist for the wedding had set up shop in the same room to keep the gorgeous blooms from wilting. We took the cakes out of their pans and started to thickly spread the key lime buttercream generously over each layer. Once all of the layers were stacked, we applied a crumb coat around the entire cake. Then we let it cool in the room for a few hours before we applied the final coat of key lime buttercream. We then picked vibrant flowers from around the island and placed them around the base of each layer of the cake.

When it was all finished, we had to transport the wedding cake on another speedboat and on the back of a Jurassic Park–style open-air truck to get it to its final destination—a Jacuzzi pool by the beach! We were both so frazzled as we tightly gripped the sides of the cake stand, making sure it didn't fall out of the back of the boat, or out of the back of the truck as we drove up and down the steepest hills on the island.

As we set up the four tiers of the key lime cake on a small table inside the Jacuzzi, standing thigh deep in water, we were able to spare a moment to take a good long look at what we had made. It was an absolutely perfect multitiered tropical-looking cake, decorated with fresh blooms from the island. We had been eaten alive by mosquitoes and survived the elements to create a dream beach confection!

Coconut Key Lime Cupcakes with Tropical Umbrellas

For a celebrity wedding on Necker Island, we baked our Coconut Key Lime cupcakes for the rehearsal dinner and a four-tier key lime wedding cake for the reception. This recipe combines both of these tropical flavors in one cupcake. If you want to bake a Coconut Key Lime cake instead, just double the recipe to make a 9-inch round four-layer key lime cake, and cover all sides with the toasted coconut flakes. Although we're partial to the cupcakes, both make wonderful desserts!

Makes 24 cupcakes

FOR THE CUPCAKES

2½ cups sifted all-purpose flour

2½ teaspoons baking powder

¼ teaspoon salt

8 tablespoons unsalted butter

1¾ cups sugar

2 large eggs

2¼ teaspoons pure vanilla extract

1¼ cups whole milk

½ cup freshly squeezed lime juice

½ cup freshly grated lime zest (5 to 6 limes)

½ cup coconut flakes

FOR THE DECORATION

1 cup coconut flakes

24 tropical paper umbrella picks

FOR THE KEY LIME CREAM CHEESE FROSTING

4 tablespoons unsalted butter

6 ounces cream cheese

4 cups sifted confectioners' sugar

½ teaspoon pure vanilla extract

½ cup freshly grated lime zest (5 to 6 limes)

½ cup coconut

For the cupcakes:

1 Preheat the oven to 350°F. Line two cupcake pans with twelve paper baking cups each.

2 Sift together the flour, baking powder, and salt, and set aside.

3 In the bowl of a stand mixer or in a bowl with a handheld electric mixer, cream together the butter and sugar for 3 to 5 minutes or until light and fluffy.

4 Add the eggs, one at a time, mixing slowly until fully incorporated.

5 Add the vanilla extract to the milk in a large liquid measuring cup.

6 Add one third of the flour mixture to the butter mixture, followed by one third of the milk mixture, and mix thoroughly until incorporated. Add another third of the flour mixture, followed by another third of the milk mixture, and mix until incorporated. Finally, add the remaining flour mixture and the remaining milk mixture, and mix until well combined. Stop to scrape down the bowl as needed.

7 Add the lime juice and zest, and mix thoroughly on low speed.

8 Fold the coconut into the batter.

9 Using a standard-size ice cream scoop, fill each baking cup so that it is two-thirds full. Bake for 16 to 18 minutes or until a toothpick inserted comes out clean. Transfer the pans to a wire rack, and let the cupcakes cool completely.

For the toasted coconut flakes:

Spread the coconut flakes evenly on a baking sheet, and toast in the oven at 350°F for 20 minutes until golden brown. Check at 10 minutes to make sure the coconut flakes toast evenly. Let cool for 10 minutes.

For the frosting:

Combine all of the ingredients in the bowl of a stand mixer or in a bowl with a handheld electric mixer. Beat until the frosting is light and airy, approximately 3 to 5 minutes. Frost the cupcakes with Georgetown Cupcake's signature swirl (see page xxv). Sprinkle with the toasted coconut flakes, garnish with the tropical paper umbrella picks, and enjoy!

Sophie's Sangria

This is a super-easy sangria to make for beach parties. We love sauvignon blanc, but you can use your favorite white wine. Or make it non-alcoholic by replacing the wine with sparkling grape juice!

2 bottles chilled white wine

½ cup chopped fresh mint leaves

2 cups sliced nectarines

2 cups sliced mangoes

4 sliced limes

2 cups fresh strawberries

Mix all ingredients in a large punch bowl or pitcher, chill for at least one hour, serve, and enjoy!

Adapting to Your Surroundings

In your professional life, there are going to be times when you are stuck in an unfamiliar environment or working situation, or are asked to do something under strenuous conditions. It could be working in a remote location without your usual tools or materials, or even finishing a project with no electricity (been there, done that!). You can't let the difficult circumstances faze you. We've been through many situations where it would have been easier to just say, "No, not possible," "It's too much trouble," or "Why should I have to work like that?" but we have never backed down from a challenge. When you are in a difficult environment and need to get something done, you need to remain professional, reach within yourself, not complain, and find a way to get it done! It will make you stronger in the end.

CHAPTER 24

Picnics

Family Picnics

When our grandparents and parents moved from Greece to Canada, many people in their villages also moved to Canada. Settling in Toronto and surrounding cities, they remained a very close-knit cultural community. Every summer, a number of the Greek villagers would meet up for reunion picnics. They were big affairs, and our whole extended family would pack up a ton of food in our red picnic coolers, drive to the park, and line up three or four long picnic tables in a row. Babee would start laying out a spread of salads, cold chicken drumsticks, and sweet treats on her red and white-checkered picnic tablecloth. We would help her set out the paper plates, plastic cups, flatware, and napkins, doing our best to keep them down while the wind blew.

When the table was all set, she would call the family around the table, as many as twenty or thirty of us, and we'd all eat and talk. Relatives and friends from the villages would come by and sit down on the benches for a while. Meanwhile, the kids would go off and play soccer and Frisbee. There was a feeling of camaraderie as we ran and played in the sunshine and the grown-ups caught up on old times back home.

how to pack for a picnic

Part of the fun of having a picnic is packing up all your food and goodies in cute wrappers so that when your picnic basket is unpacked, everyone *ooh*s and *aah*s at how cool everything looks. Here are some fun ways to wrap some typical picnic items:

• Bundle all your silverware (or disposable flatware) in colorful paper napkins, and wrap with baker's twine.

• Try using biodegradable bamboo plates instead of Styrofoam plates. They make food look even more appetizing (and are better for the environment).

• Wrap sandwiches in parchment or fun checkered or patterned wax paper, and tie with baker's twine.

• Put together "lunch boxes" for each guest, and wrap each component in wax paper and baker's twine. ✪

Cherry Cupcake Tarts

Sometimes Babee would bring chilled tarts to the village picnics—butter pecan, lemon, and apple—but cherry was our favorite. She used to serve all of her tarts uncovered, with the filling exposed, but we tweaked her recipe and have added decorative flaky tops. These are yummy served cold or hot from the oven!

Makes 24 cupcake tarts

FOR THE FILLING

5 cups pitted cherries

1 cup sugar

2 tablespoons sifted cornstarch

¼ teaspoon salt

¼ teaspoon pure vanilla extract

FOR THE CUPCAKE TARTS

1½ cups sifted all-purpose flour

5 tablespoons sugar

16 tablespoons unsalted butter (make sure it is very cold)

¼ teaspoon salt

10 tablespoons cold water

round cookie cutter, 4 inches in diameter

round cookie cutter, 3 inches in diameter

cookie cutters in artistic shapes, such as
  hearts or stars, 1 inch or less in diameter

serrated pizza wheel (optional)

2 large egg yolks

½ cup heavy cream

For the filling:

In a small saucepan over medium heat, heat the cherries, sugar, cornstarch, and salt. Mix in the vanilla extract, stirring for 2 to 3 minutes. Remove from heat and let cool to room temperature.

For the cupcake tarts:

❶ Preheat the oven to 400°F. Grease two cupcake pans with butter (no need for paper baking cups), and set aside.

2 Add the flour, sugar, butter, and salt to a food processor, and pulse for approximately 30 seconds or until the mixture forms a crumble.

3 Add the water slowly, and pulse until the mixture is a moist crumble. Carefully empty the dough mixture out onto a clean surface covered in flour, and fold the dough into a ball. Wrap it in parchment paper or plastic wrap, and place it in the refrigerator to chill for approximately 1 hour.

4 Remove the dough from the refrigerator, and using a rolling pin, roll it out into a flat sheet, approximately ½ inch thick.

5 Using a round cookie cutter 4 inches in diameter, cut out twenty-four small dough rounds. Place each round in a well of the cupcake pans, and press to conform it to the shape of the well. Fold over the excess dough, and use a fork to press and pattern the edges of each crust. Using a fork, poke holes in the bottom of each crust. Place the cupcake pans in the refrigerator to chill for at least 30 minutes.

6 Using the remaining dough, cut out twenty-four smaller rounds using a round cookie cutter 3 inches in diameter. Using cookie cutters of various shapes, cut out artistic designs in each dough round, forming a little window to expose the filling. If desired, cut out strips of dough using a serrated pizza wheel. Place all of these rounds on a cookie sheet lined with parchment paper, and place in the refrigerator for at least 30 minutes.

7 Using a standard-size ice cream scoop, transfer the cooled cherry filling to each well in the cupcake pans.

8 Place one 3-inch dough round on top of each cupcake tart to cover the cherry filling.

9 Beat together the egg yolks and heavy cream to form an egg wash. Using a pastry brush, gently brush each top dough round with a thin layer of the egg wash.

10 Bake for 30 minutes or until cherry juices start bubbling. Serve hot or cold.

CHAPTER 25

Sporting Events

Football Parties!

The Super Bowl is probably the most popular sporting event in the country, and it's also a great opportunity to entertain! The 2012 Super Bowl turned out to be extra special for us: one of the teams playing in the championship game was from New York, where we were about to open a new Georgetown Cupcake (in SoHo), and the other team was from New England, where we were opening a new shop later that spring (in Boston). We were already offering special Super Bowl–themed cupcakes in all of our bakeries, but we had to do more . . . we simply had to throw a party in our Big Apple apartment!

Super Bowl parties and sporting event parties are different from formal dinner parties. Rather than plan a structured dinner with separate courses, we simply wanted

to ensure a steady supply of snacks and good old-fashioned guy-friendly comfort food. We wanted to serve the usual game-time snacks like chips and popcorn but make them a bit more special than a store-bought bag emptied into a bowl. Several of our friends were planning on stopping by at various times throughout the evening to say hello and catch part of the game, so we also needed a menu that appealed to everyone and that was flexible enough to allow visitors to eat at different times.

For the snacks, we decided to make our own potato chips. We sliced a bunch of potatoes into thin discs, lightly salted them, drizzled them in olive oil, and then baked them in the oven.

For the main course, we decided to make a large pot of turkey chili, a perfect dish because it is hearty, can be made in large quantities, and gets better and better after reheating. It's also healthy even though it feels like game-day food. First, we cubed up a few pounds of fresh turkey breast, seasoned it with salt, pepper, and cayenne pepper, and then browned it in a pan. Then we combined it in a large pot with chopped onions, two different types of beans, plum tomatoes, and minced garlic. We let it simmer slowly for a couple of hours and served it along with a toppings bar that included sour cream, shredded cheddar cheese, chopped jalapeño peppers, tortilla chips, and fresh-baked crusty bread. The chili was a huge hit, and there was more than enough to feed everyone.

Then, while all the guys were still watching the game, we shifted gears to dessert. We're not huge football fanatics—watching the last quarter is usually enough for us—so during the first three quarters, we went back to the kitchen to work on our football-themed cupcakes. We baked chocolate peanut butter chip cupcakes and piped on green buttercream to resemble the grass on the field. We carefully piped white goal lines on the grass. Then we cut out the shape of a jersey in fondant, in each team's respective colors, and decorated them with the numbers of their respective star players, Tom Brady and Eli Manning. To top it off, we added fondant footballs and goalposts. We arranged the "team" cupcakes on a tray and brought them out during the final quarter. Believe it or not, the display actually caused the diehard fans to take their eyes off the screen for a moment! Guests took a cupcake (some took two!) representing the team they were rooting for. Since we were getting ready to open our Georgetown Cupcake shop in SoHo, we knew to make extra Giants cupcakes, and those were definitely the most popular!

The last quarter was very exciting, with several lead changes and big plays that kept everyone in the room glued to their seats. In the end, the Giants won the game in the final minutes. We could hear cars honking outside and crowds of cheering New Yorkers spilling out of bars and restaurants onto the streets, celebrating the victory. We loved this town already!

Chocolate Peanut Butter Chip Football and Team Jersey Cupcakes

This recipe is great for a sports party, and the fondant jerseys give the cupcakes an extra-personal touch!

Makes 18 cupcakes

FOR THE CUPCAKES

1¼ cups sifted all-purpose flour

½ teaspoon baking soda

¼ teaspoon salt

8 tablespoons unsalted butter

1¼ cups sugar

2 large eggs

1¼ teaspoons pure vanilla extract

1 cup whole milk

½ cup peanut butter chips

½ cup sifted cocoa powder

FOR THE FROSTING

16 tablespoons unsalted butter

4 cups sifted confectioners' sugar

1 teaspoon whole milk

1 teaspoon pure vanilla extract

⅛ teaspoon salt

½ teaspoon green gel food color

FOR THE DECORATION

¼ pound fondant in the team colors

number-shaped cookie cutters

piping gel

For the cupcakes:

1 Preheat the oven to 350°F. Line a cupcake pan with twelve paper baking cups and a second pan with six baking cups.

2 Sift together the flour, baking soda, and salt in a bowl, and set aside.

3 Cream together the butter and sugar on medium speed until light and fluffy, for 3 to 5 minutes.

4 Add the eggs one at a time, mixing slowly after each addition.

Katherine Kallinis Berman & Sophie Kallinis LaMontagne

5 Combine the vanilla extract and milk in a large liquid measuring cup.

6 Add one third of the flour mixture to the butter mixture, then gradually add one third of the milk mixture, beating slowly until well incorporated. Add another third of the flour mixture, followed by another third of the milk mixture. Stop to scrape down the bowl as needed. Add the remaining flour mixture, followed by the remaining milk mixture, and beat just until combined.

7 Add the peanut butter chips and cocoa powder, beating on low speed until just incorporated.

8 Using a standard-size ice cream scoop, fill each baking cup so that it is two-thirds full. Bake for 18 to 20 minutes (start checking at 15 minutes) or until a toothpick inserted into the center of a cupcake comes out clean. Cool completely.

For the frosting:

1 Place all of the ingredients in the bowl of a stand mixer or in a bowl with a handheld electric mixer. Beat until well incorporated and the frosting is light and fluffy, approximately 3 to 5 minutes.

2 Place the frosting in a piping bag fitted with a multi-opening "grass" tip. To create a buttercream grass surface on top of each cupcake, hold the piping bag ⅛ inch from the surface of the cupcake. Squeeze and pull up in quick short strokes, creating a short level of grass. Repeat until the entire surface of the cupcake is covered.

To make the fondant football jerseys:

Roll out flat pieces of fondant about ¼ inch thick in the team colors. Using a scalpel, cut out eighteen football jersey shapes. Next, cut out your favorite players' numbers in complementary team colors using cookie cutters, and attach them to the jerseys using piping gel or water. Place a fondant jersey on each cupcake, serve, and enjoy!

Part 5

DC CUPCAKES' BIGGEST BASHES

On DC Cupcakes, *we throw some super-sweet bashes! Check out what happens behind the scenes. . . .*

CHAPTER ⊚ 26

Behind the Scenes

DC Cupcakes' Biggest Bashes

The year 2011 was a monumental one both for our family and for Georgetown Cupcake. Not only did we celebrate a wedding and a sixtieth birthday, but we also broke a world record and took the Big Apple by storm! All of these celebrations were captured on *DC Cupcakes,* but here are some behind-the-scenes moments you *didn't* see!

My Sweet Wedding

My wedding planning process was truly a family affair and, consequently, full of drama! I absolutely loved the gorgeous bridal shower that Mommy and Sophie threw for me, but I did notice some stress on Sophie's face. That's because she had put

Mommy in charge of the guest list and seating plan. Mommy decided not to write down last names on her guest list. Being Greek, we have at least ten Helens, ten Marys, and ten Annas in our extended family. So on the morning of the shower, Sophie was desperately trying to help Mommy sort out the seating chart with less than an hour before all the guests were set to arrive. Needless to say, the seating became somewhat of a free-for-all!

On my wedding day, everything seemed to be going according to plan . . . until I slipped on my dress. It barely fit! The seamstress had taken it in too much during the last fitting, and the zipper wouldn't move! But after having my ribs squeezed together and multiple hands trying to fit me in the dress, the zipper finally went up. Thank goodness! Or at least that's what I thought at the time.

During the signing of the *ketubah* (the wedding contract), which happens right before the ceremony in a Jewish wedding, I turned to Sophie and told her I wasn't feeling well. "I think I'm going to faint!" I whispered.

Sure enough, I did. When I came to, I could tell everyone was freaked out!

I knew that everyone was worried I was going to faint again while going down the aisle. Sharon Sacks, my wedding planner, rushed to get me some orange juice, while

everyone anxiously looked at their watches. We were running fifteen minutes behind because of my fainting spell. We decided to unzip my dress a few inches and send me down the aisle, fingers crossed. I was in too much of a daze to even care at that point if the back of my gown was hanging open. I don't think anyone really noticed—but if you go back and watch the episode, you can spot it!

—*Katherine*

Lemon and Fig Cupcakes
One thing that didn't get shown very much on *DC Cupcakes* was the magnificent kitchen in which I got to bake Katherine's wedding cupcake tower with our Georgetown Cupcake staff. We were lucky enough to be able to use the kitchen at Saint Barbara Greek Orthodox Church in Santa Barbara, California. The kitchen at the church was on a rolling hillside overlooking the Pacific Ocean. Every day we baked with the kitchen door open, letting in the fresh air and sunshine. The kitchen opened up onto a patio that overlooked an orchard of lemon and fig trees. Being from the East Coast, we were thrilled to be able to pick the fruit right off the trees and eat it! Mommy absolutely loves figs (she is Greek, after all), so one day after lunch we surprised her by making these cupcakes. They are beautiful to serve without frosting, but if you want to top them, we suggest a vanilla cream cheese frosting (page 154, without the rum).

Makes 24 cupcakes

FOR THE CUPCAKES
2½ cups sifted all-purpose flour
2½ teaspoons baking powder
¼ teaspoon salt
8 tablespoons unsalted butter
1¾ cups sugar
2 large eggs

2¼ teaspoons pure vanilla extract
1¼ cups whole milk
½ cup freshly squeezed lemon juice
½ cup freshly grated lemon zest (from
 approximately 2 to 3 lemons)
½ cup fresh or dried figs, sliced

For the cupcakes:

1 Preheat the oven to 350°F. Line two cupcake pans with twelve paper baking cups each.

2 Sift together the flour, baking powder, and salt in a bowl, and set aside.

3 In the bowl of a stand mixer or in a bowl with a handheld electric mixer, cream together the butter and sugar until light and fluffy, approximately 3 to 5 minutes.

4 Add the eggs one at a time, mixing slowly after each addition.

5 Combine the vanilla extract and milk in a large liquid measuring cup.

6 Add one third of the flour mixture to the butter mixture, then gradually add one third of the milk mixture, beating slowly until well incorporated. Add another third of the flour mixture, followed by another third of the milk mixture. Stop to scrape down the bowl as needed. Add the remaining flour mixture, followed by the remaining milk mixture, and beat just until combined.

7 Add the lemon juice and lemon zest, and mix until well combined.

8 Scoop batter into the baking cups so that each is two-thirds full. On top of each cupcake, place one fig slice so that it covers the surface of the batter. Bake for 15 to 18 minutes or until a toothpick inserted into the center of a cupcake comes out clean. Transfer the pans to a wire rack to cool completely. Serve and enjoy!

Recipe for Success

The Importance of Delegating

$\mathcal{K}$atherine and Ben decided to have a small wedding party with only a best man (Ben's brother) and me, Katherine's matron of honor. We are very close, so I was honored to take on this role, but she also left me without any reinforcements. I had nobody (well, except Mommy) to turn to when planning the shower. In retrospect, I wish I had enlisted the help of my aunts and cousins and gotten them to pitch in with tasks such as addressing invitations, setting up the cupcake bar, and helping seat people once the guests arrived. This would have saved me a lot of stress on the day of the shower, and things may have gone a little more smoothly. You live and you learn!

—*Sophie*

Nutcracker Sweet

We are big fans of the Washington Ballet, and we've been providing cupcakes for their annual Nutcracker Tea Party at the historic Willard Hotel ever since we've been open. All the little ballerinas come straight from their performance to a whimsically decorated room full of sweets and tea! It's the perfect holiday event for families in the Washington, DC, area.

So in 2011, when they asked us to build a giant Nutcracker out of cupcakes, we naturally said yes. But as we were finalizing the design, one thing had us stumped: how would we re-create his fluffy white beard? Then it hit us: cotton candy! We went out to buy a cotton candy machine, but when we turned it on, it wasn't working. We spun it round and round, but nothing happened. Then, after a few minutes, the first wisps

of cotton candy sugar started to appear. We were mesmerized! We must have watched it in amazement for over an hour without doing any actual work. We just kept grabbing the cotton candy as it appeared and munching away at it.

But our cotton candy binge wasn't our biggest problem. We were also conducting employee interviews in our workspace, and needed to push the Nutcracker to one side so we could have more room. As Sophie was rolling her half of the Nutcracker, she hit the edge of the fireplace and he fell face first into it. We had to take off all the cupcakes and redo him. It was frustrating, but we got it done in the nick of time, and all the children loved him.

White Chocolate Peppermint Cupcakes

Makes 24 cupcakes

FOR THE CUPCAKES

2½ cups sifted all-purpose flour

2½ teaspoons baking powder

¼ teaspoon salt

8 tablespoons unsalted butter

1¾ cups sugar

2 large eggs

2¼ teaspoons pure peppermint extract

1¼ cups whole milk

1 cup crushed white chocolate peppermint bark
(page 157, but do not include dark chocolate
if you want cupcakes to be purely white
chocolate)

FOR THE FROSTING

16 tablespoons unsalted butter

4 cups sifted confectioners' sugar

1 teaspoon whole milk

1 teaspoon pure vanilla extract

⅛ teaspoon salt

¼ cup cooled melted white chocolate

1 teaspoon pure peppermint extract

no-taste red food color, to line piping bag

For the cupcakes:

1 Preheat the oven to 350°F. Line two cupcake pans with twelve paper baking cups each.

2 Sift together the flour, baking powder, and salt, and set aside.

3 In the bowl of a stand mixer or in a bowl with a handheld electric mixer, cream together the butter and sugar for 3 to 5 minutes or until light and fluffy.

4 Add the eggs, one at a time, mixing slowly until fully incorporated.

5 Add the peppermint extract to the milk in a large liquid measuring cup.

6 Add one third of the flour mixture to the butter mixture, followed by one third of the milk mixture, and mix thoroughly on low speed. Add another third of the flour mixture and another third of the milk mixture, and mix thoroughly. Add the final third of the flour mixture, followed by the final third of the milk mixture, and mix until well combined. Stop to scrape down the bowl as needed.

7 Add crushed peppermint bark, and mix into the batter on low speed.

8 Using a standard-size ice cream scoop, fill each baking cup so that it is two-thirds full. Bake for 16 to 18 minutes or until a toothpick inserted comes out clean. Transfer the pans to a wire rack, and let the cupcakes cool completely.

For the frosting:

1 Add all of the ingredients, except the red food color, to the bowl of a stand mixer or a bowl with a handheld electric mixer. Beat until frosting is light and airy, approximately 3 to 5 minutes.

2 Using a straw, streak a single line of red food color on the inside of the piping bag, from the bottom of the bag to the top. Repeat two or three more times on other sides of the bag.

3 Add the frosting to the bag, and frost each cupcake with a signature swirl (see page xxv) to get a cool "candy cane" effect.

One stripe of color along piping bag.

Two stripes of color along piping bag.

Three stripes of color along piping bag.

One Ton Cupcake

Baking the world's largest cupcake is literally the biggest challenge we have ever taken on. We decided that we really wanted to put Georgetown Cupcake on the map and break the existing record for the world's largest cupcake. We didn't want to just break the record, though; we wanted to *shatter* it. The previous world record holder weighed over 1,300 pounds, so we wanted to bake a cupcake that weighed over *one ton*! Mommy, who is usually our biggest cheerleader, was convinced we couldn't do it, but we pressed on with our plan.

We rented a huge oven from Michigan that is normally used to treat auto parts, and had a custom pan built that was four feet tall and five feet across. The oven was so big that we had to put it outside in our parking lot! We filled the pan with nearly 2,500 pounds of chocolate cupcake batter, which took a full day to mix.

After baking the cupcake for over twenty-four hours and then letting it cool for another twenty-four hours, we were getting ready to remove it from the pan when it sprang a leak! The cupcake had not fully cooled, and there was batter deep in the center that was actually still baking, even when we removed it from the oven. So we quickly rebolted the pan and let the cupcake cool another twenty-four hours.

Everyone was so worried. "Give up!" Mommy pleaded with us. Even Steve, always the voice of calm, was at a loss for words. All of his careful calculations were called into question, and he didn't know whether the cupcake would hold together. Surprisingly, it was Sophie who bolstered everyone's spirits and calmly assured us that the cupcake just needed to cool down. And in the end, she was right!

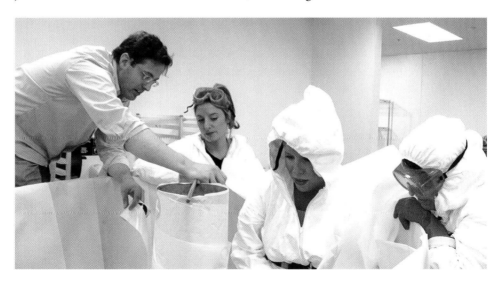

What wasn't shown on *DC Cupcakes* was Mommy's hilarious lecture to the rest of the baking staff about how our giant cupcake was actually a model of how the universe was created. It was hard for everyone to keep a straight face while listening to Mommy quote Stephen Hawking and liken the hot batter in the center of our cupcake to the lava at the core of the planet Earth.

In the end, we baked and frosted a cupcake that weighed 2,594 pounds and set a new Guinness World Record for the world's largest cupcake. Georgetown Cupcake officially went down in history! To celebrate this achievement, we held a block party with our staff and neighbors and all dug into the giant cupcake. We brought in balloons and even had T-shirts made that said "I ate the World's Largest Cupcake . . . and I'm full!"

Recipe for Success

When the Going Gets Tough, the Tough Keep Going!

Sometimes you're working on something and it's not going the way you thought it would. You may get extremely discouraged and just want to throw in the towel. If we learned one thing from baking the world's biggest cupcake, it's this: you can't let a slight setback (or, in our case, a giant one!) derail your plans. Maybe you'll have to start from scratch and do it all over again. Maybe you'll have to regroup, rethink, and retry.

The question is, how bad do you want it? Are you willing to see it through? There is a solution to every problem, though it may not be apparent at first. Just keep a positive attitude, ignore your critics, and stay on your path. Even if—in our case—your path is leaking chocolate batter! If we had given up, we never would have broken the world record. We knew we could, and we refused to believe anything else.

The World Record–Setting One Ton Cupcake

When we set out to bake the world's largest cupcake, we had no idea how hard it was going to be. The criteria were tough—the cupcake had to be baked as one solid piece, it had to have the proper ratio of frosting to cupcake (to make it a cupcake and not a cake), it had to be able to stand outside of the pan once it was baked, and it had to be completely edible. What goes in a one ton cupcake? Check it out below!

Makes 1 one ton cupcake

500 pounds flour	750 pounds sugar
300 pounds butter	200 dozen eggs
300 pounds milk	100 pounds cocoa powder

As for the frosting, we used more than 100 pounds of butter and 500 pounds of confectioners' sugar. We used giant jawbreakers as our "sprinkles" for the top, and finished it off with a giant paper cupcake wrapper emblazoned with Georgetown Cupcake stickers!

Mommy's Birthday Bash

Mommy's sixtieth birthday was a night to remember! Since we weren't able to take her to Greece, we decided to bring Greece to her in the form of an authentic Greek celebration with dancing, singing, live donkeys and pigs, and a lamb roasting over an open flame, all at a nearby barn.

We invited all of her family and friends, and we even bought togas for everyone to wear as well as Greek flags to wave. When we walked Mommy in, she was completely shocked!

Poochie even came along to join the party. But sometime during the dinner and dancing, he got loose and took off across the open fields like a free bird. Steve had to chase after him in his Greek toga before finally grabbing him in a bear hug more than three hundred yards away!

The party was amazing—we had tons of food and tons of cupcakes, and broke lots of plates—and Mommy loved the Greek goddess statue of her that we made with over a thousand cupcakes!

Recipe for Success

Embrace Your Heritage

~~~~~~

*W*hen we were growing up, especially as teens, we didn't necessarily think that all of the Greek traditions that Babee and Mommy were trying to teach us were very cool. In fact, we thought a lot of them were kind of strange. It wasn't until we were older that we realized what an important part of our life our culture was, and now, more than ever, we do our best to keep our Greek traditions alive, especially when we're planning parties or celebrations.

Babee's Greek Walnut Spice Cupcakes

Makes 24 cupcakes

2 cups sifted all-purpose flour

3 teaspoons baking powder

1 teaspoon ground cinnamon

½ teaspoon ground cloves

8 tablespoons unsalted butter

¾ cup granulated sugar

5 large eggs

½ cup whole milk

2 teaspoons orange juice

2 cups ground walnuts

confectioners' sugar, for dusting

1 Preheat the oven to 350°F, and line two cupcake pans with twelve paper baking cups each.

2 Sift together the flour, baking powder, cinnamon, and cloves in a bowl, and set aside.

3 In the bowl of a stand mixer or in a bowl with a handheld electric mixer, cream together the butter and granulated sugar until light and fluffy, approximately 3 to 5 minutes.

4 Add the eggs, one at a time, mixing slowly after each addition.

5 Add one third of the flour mixture to the butter mixture, followed by one third of the milk, and mix slowly. Add another third of the flour mixture, followed by another third of the milk, and mix thoroughly. Add the final third of the flour mixture, followed by the final third of the milk, and mix until just combined. Stop as needed to scrape down the sides of the bowl.

6 Add orange juice and walnuts, and mix until just combined.

7 Using a standard-size ice cream scoop, fill each baking cup so that it is two-thirds full, and bake for 18 to 20 minutes or until a toothpick inserted comes out clean.

8 When cupcakes have cooled, dust with confectioners' sugar and serve!

DC Cupcakes *Takes New York*

The process of opening our new shop in SoHo was a high-stress marathon from start to finish. Not only were we doing our renovation in one of the most heavily regulated types of historic buildings in New York City, but we were also working alongside our landlord, who was in the process of renovating the entire building. On the day before we opened, the building literally had no front and no rear! The storefront was delivered and installed in the nick of time, but we didn't quite finish everything. On the night of our opening party, the back of our space had no roof— the landlord was planning on installing a skylight, but it wasn't ready in time, so there was a big blue painter's tarp over the rear of the building, where the roof should have been. Since it was February, it was so cold inside that we had to plug in space heaters to keep everyone and everything warm, including the cupcakes! On top of that, we had to train all of our new employees and decided to hold a last-minute cupcake boot camp to show them the ropes. But in the end, we managed to pull it all off and open on time. In fact, we had a fantastic grand opening! As we like to say about New York—if we can *bake* it here, we can *bake* it anywhere!

First Impressions Count

$\mathcal{N}$ew York is a big city, and it's difficult to make a splash. We wanted to put our best foot forward so that anyone walking into Georgetown Cupcake SoHo for the first time would be blown away and—we hoped—tell ten of their friends to check it out. We worked really hard to throw an amazing opening party and have a fabulous opening weekend, greeting each customer coming through the door with a free cupcake, all day long. Everyone who came in loved it. No matter what business you are in, it's always important to show your customers care, quality, and consistency. You want them to feel welcome and appreciated, and you want the experience to be an enjoyable one. We love it when we see people walk out of Georgetown Cupcake with smiles on their faces carrying a bright pink box filled with our finest cupcakes!

Big Apple Crumble Cupcakes

We developed this flavor to celebrate our grand opening in the "Big Apple." We used Gala apples, but feel free to use your own favorites! If you like, for an extra-special touch, you can cut an apple shape (using a mini apple-shaped cookie cutter) out of red fondant, and top each cupcake with a fondant apple.

Makes 18 cupcakes

FOR THE CRUMBLE

3½ tablespoons granulated sugar

1 cup sifted all-purpose flour

2 teaspoons ground cinnamon

6 tablespoons cold butter, diced into small cubes

½ cup light brown sugar

FOR THE CUPCAKES

2½ cups sifted all-purpose flour

3 teaspoons baking powder

1 teaspoon ground cinnamon

½ teaspoon salt

16 tablespoons unsalted butter

2 cups granulated sugar

4 large eggs

⅓ cup hot water

2½ cups freshly grated apples (4 to 5 medium apples)

FOR THE CINNAMON BUTTERCREAM FROSTING

16 tablespoons unsalted butter

4 cups confectioners' sugar

1 teaspoon whole milk

⅛ teaspoon salt

1 teaspoon ground cinnamon

¼ teaspoon pure vanilla extract

For the crumble:

1 Preheat the oven to 350°F.

2 In a medium mixing bowl, combine all of the ingredients, and mix together using your fingertips. Spread the crumb mixture on a cookie sheet lined with parchment paper, and bake for 30 minutes or until the crumble reaches a golden brown color. Let cool and set aside. Leave the oven on to bake the cupcakes.

◎ Katherine Kallinis Berman & Sophie Kallinis LaMontagne

For the cupcakes:

1 Line a cupcake pan with twelve paper baking cups and a second pan with six baking cups.

2 Sift together the flour, baking powder, cinnamon, and salt, and set aside.

3 In the bowl of a stand mixer or in a bowl with a handheld electric mixer, cream together the butter and sugar until light and fluffy, approximately 3 to 5 minutes.

4 Add the eggs one at a time, mixing slowly after each addition.

5 Add one third of the flour mixture to the butter mixture, then gradually add one third of the hot water, beating slowly until well incorporated. Add another third of the flour mixture, followed by a third of the hot water. Add the remaining flour mixture, followed by the remaining hot water, and beat just until combined. Stop to scrape down the bowl as needed.

6 Using a spatula, fold the grated apple and half of the apple crumble mixture into the batter.

7 Using a standard-size ice cream scoop, fill each baking cup so that it is two-thirds full. Bake for 18 to 20 minutes (start checking at 15 minutes) or until a toothpick inserted into the center of a cupcake comes out clean. After 5 minutes, transfer the cupcakes to a wire rack to cool completely for approximately 20 minutes.

For the frosting:

Place all ingredients in the bowl of a stand mixer or in a bowl with a handheld electric mixer. Beat until the frosting is light and airy, approximately 3 to 5 minutes. Frost each cupcake with a signature swirl (see page xxv), and top with a sprinkling of the remaining apple crumble.

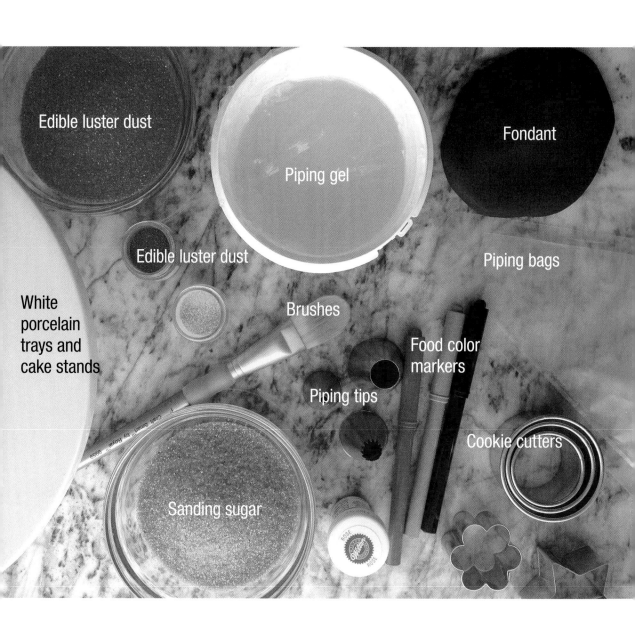

Edible luster dust

Piping gel

Fondant

Edible luster dust

Piping bags

White
porcelain
trays and
cake stands

Brushes

Food color
markers

Piping tips

Cookie cutters

Sanding sugar

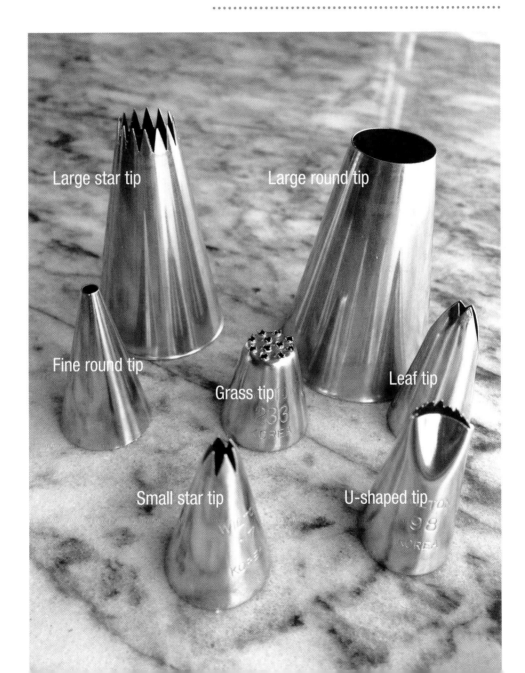

Large star tip

Large round tip

Fine round tip

Grass tip

Leaf tip

Small star tip

U-shaped tip

CREDITS

Grateful acknowledgment is given to the following for the use of their photographs in this publication.

All photographs other than those listed below are copyright © Dayna Smith.

Ben Berman: 250
Katherine Kallinis Berman: xvi, xxvi, 8, 9, 10, 25, 43, 45, 55, 64, 73, 77, 83, 85, 89 *(left),* 92, 99, 106, 116, 117, 121, 129, 138, 143, 146, 148, 160, 163, 165, 184, 186, 188, 196, 197, 199, 205, 207, 210, 220, 222–23, 228, 234, 236, 239, 245, 255, 260, 267, 268, 273

Sophie Kallinis LaMontagne: 12, 13, 15, 40, 93, 150, 170, 176, 208, 242
Elizabeth Messina: i, xxi *(right),* 30, 33, 34, 41, 71, 202, 252, 253
Hudson Taylor: 42, 47
TLC: 127, 139, 261, 263, 264, 265
TLC/Keir Johnson: 257
TLC/George Lange: iv
TLC/Walling McGarity: xviii, 173
Michelle Thiesen: 167 *(large photograph)*
Sara Jaye Weiss/Startraks Photo: 68, 269
Courtesy of the authors: 58, 59, 105, 111, 120, 166–67, 180, 191, 200, 201, 212, 238, 244, 274

Note: A list of full recipe names by type, along with celebration themes, can be found in the front of the book.

Almond Easter Bunny Cupcakes, 90–93
Angel Food Mini Cupcake Flag, 128–29
Apple Crumble Cupcakes, 268, 270–71

baking tips, xxii–xxiv, 159
Banana Chocolate Chip Monkey Cupcakes, 6–9
basket cupcake wrappers, 89
Blackberry Cupcakes with Lemon Filling, 182–85
blueberries, 128–29, 139
Blueberry Cheesecake Cupcakes with Blueberry
      Compote, 206–7
Blue Velvet Cupcakes, Star of David, 164–65
Bunny Cupcakes, Almond Easter, 90–93
butter, xxiii
Butter Cookies, 86, 98–99
buttercream frosting
    baby blue/pink reveal, 62–65
    champagne, 38–39
    cinnamon, 194
    lavender, 24–25
    mixing and matching, 13
    mocha, 52–53
    orange/lime, 134–35, 221, 222
    pink, 174–75
    raspberry, 14–15
    roses, 112–13
    salted caramel, 74
    storing, 173
    sunflowers, 116
    vanilla, 62–64, 122, 136–37, 224–25, 246, 247

Cake, New Year's, 70, 72–73
candied flowers, 101
Candy Bar Cupcakes, 134–35
candy decorations, 132, 144, 145

Caramel-/Chocolate-Drizzled Popcorn, 177
Caramel Pop Rocks Cupcakes, Chocolate Salted,
      74–77
carrot icing, 97
centerpieces, 205
Champagne Cupcakes, 38–41
Cheddar and Marmalade Tea Sandwiches, 187
Cheesecake Cupcakes with Blueberry Compote,
      206–7
Cherry Cupcake Tarts, 236, 240–41
chocolate
    in Campfire Cupcakes, 214
    choosing, xxiii
    ganache frosting, 7–8, 18–19, 106, 112,
      114, 137
    in "Hamburger" Cupcakes, 122–23
    Ice Cream Cone Cupcakes, 224–25, 226
    in Marble Mini Cupcakes, 44–45
    pailleté sprinkles, 101
    spiderwebs, 137
    white, 94–96, 157–59, 177, 221–23, 258–60
Chocolate Chip Monkey Cupcakes, Banana, 6–9
Chocolate-Drizzled Popcorn, Caramel-, 177
Chocolate Eggnog Cupcakes, 150, 154–56
Chocolate Espresso Layered Cupcakes, 52–53
Chocolate Hazelnut Cupcake, 18–19
Chocolate Mini Egg Cupcakes, White, 94–96
Chocolate Peanut Butter Chip Cupcakes, 206,
      245–46
Chocolate Peppermint Bark, 157–59
Chocolate Peppermint Cupcakes, White, 258–60
Chocolate Salted Caramel Pop Rocks Cupcakes,
      74–77
Christmas Ornament Chocolate Eggnog Cupcakes,
      150, 154–56

cinnamon, 198–99, 270–71

Cinnamon Cupcake, Honey, and Yogurt Parfaits, Greek, 194–96

Citrus Orange/Lime Icy Cupcake Pops, 218, 221–23, 226

cocoa powder, xxiii, 154, 155, 214

Coconut Key Lime Cupcakes, 228, 232–33

coconut macaroons, 106

Coke Floats, 226–27

confectioners' sugar dusting, 50

confetti, edible, 100

cookies, 84–85, 98–99, 106, 157–59

Cotton Candy Cupcakes with Fondant Pillows, 174–76

cranberry juice, 28, 139

Cranberry Orange Cupcakes, Whole Wheat, 54–55

Cranberry Spice "Turkey" Cupcakes, 144–45

cream cheese frosting, 13, 144, 154–55, 164–65, 232–33, 254

Cucumber and Cream Cheese Tea Sandwiches, 186

cupcake liners, xxii–xxiii, 12

cupcake picks, 216

cupcake pops, 221–23, 224

cupcake tower, 35

Decorate-Your-Own Cupcake Bar, 16–17

decorations
  buttercream flowers, 112–13, 116
  candy, 132, 144–45
  cupcakes as, 43, 205
  dusting, 50
  edible fresh flowers, 117
  luster dust, 154, 155
  mixing and matching, 13
  spiderwebs, 137
  staples of, 272
  toppings guide, 100–101
  See also fondant; frosting

dragées, 100

Ducky Cupcakes, Yellow, 62–65

Earl Grey Teacake Cupcakes, Lavender, 24–25

Easter Bunny Cupcakes, Almond, 90–93

Egg Cupcakes in Egg Cartons, 94–96

Eggnog Cupcakes, 154–56

Espresso Layered Cupcakes, 52–53

favors, 36–37

Fig Cupcakes, Lemon and, 254–55

Floats, Old-Fashioned Coke, 226–27

flour, xxiii

Flowerpot with Honeybee Yogurt Cupcakes, 108, 112–15

flowers, edible, 101, 117

fondant
  Christmas ornament, 150, 154, 156
  cotton candy–stuffed pillows, 174–76
  ducks, 62, 64–65
  Easter bunnies, 90–93
  Easter eggs, 94–96
  honeybee, 108, 112
  leaves, 114
  monkey faces, 8–9
  monograms, 38, 39
  monster faces, 136–38
  peaches, 192–93
  roses, 38–41
  sports jersey/football, 245–47
  Star of David, 164–65
  turkeys, 143–45
  working with, 10

frosting
  blackberry, 182, 184
  chocolate ganache, 7–8, 18–19, 106, 112, 114, 137
  cinnamon, 270–71
  cream cheese, 13, 144, 154–55, 164–65, 232–33, 254
  ginger, 192–93
  marshmallow, 214–16
  mixing and matching, 13
  piping tips, 97, 260, 273
  signature swirl, xxv

white chocolate peppermint, 258–60
See also buttercream frosting
frozen desserts, 118, 220–25

ganache, chocolate, 7–8, 18–19, 106, 112, 114, 137
Giant Chocolate Hazelnut Cupcake, 18–19
Ginger Peach Cupcakes, 192–93
glaze, citrus, 54–55
gold leaf, 50, 74, 76, 101
graham cracker bottoms, 214
grapes/grape juice, 28, 139, 234
Greek recipes
    Cinnamon Cupcake, Honey, and Yogurt
        Parfaits, 194–96
    Kolokithopita, 146–47
    Koulourakia, 98–99
    Loukoumades, 198–99
    Vasilopita, 70, 72–73
    Walnut Spice Cupcakes, 266–67

"Hamburger" Cupcakes, 122–23
Hazelnut Cupcake, Giant Chocolate, 18–19
honey, 7, 147, 198–99, 205
Honey, and Yogurt Parfaits, Cinnamon Cupcake,
    194–95
Honeybee Yogurt Cupcakes, 108, 112–15
hostess gifts, 107

Ice Cream Cone Cupcakes, 224
ice cream floats, 226–27
ice cream shakes, strawberry, 121
Iced Tea, Peach Nectar, 197

jimmies, 100

Key Lime Cupcakes, Coconut, 228, 232–33
Kolokithopita (Greek Pumpkin Phyllo Pastries),
    146–47
Koulourakia (Greek Butter Cookies), 86, 98–99

Lavender Earl Grey Teacake Cupcakes, 24–25
layered desserts, 52–53, 74–77, 80–83, 194–96

Lemon and Fig Cupcakes, 254–55
lemon filling, 182–85
licorice, 112, 114
Lime Cupcakes, Coconut Key, 228, 232–33
Lime Icy Cupcake Pops, 218, 221–23, 226
Loukoumades, Greek, 198–99
luster dust, 112, 114, 154, 155

Macaroons, Passover, 106
mangoes, 234
Marble Mini Cupcakes, 44–45
Marmalade Tea Sandwiches, Cheddar, 187
marshmallow, working with, 213
Marshmallow Campfire Cupcakes, 214–16
measurement conversion table, xxiv
meze, 69–70
Milk Shakes, Strawberry, 121
Mini Cupcake Flag, Angel Food, 128–29
Mini Cupcakes, Marble, 44–45
mint, 157–59, 197, 234, 258–60
mocha buttercream frosting, 52–53
"Mocktails," Pink, 28
Monkey Cupcakes, Banana Chocolate
    Chip, 6–9
monograms, fondant, 38, 39
Monster Cupcakes, Tie-Dyed, 136–38

nectarines, 234
nonpareils, 100, 154

One Ton Cupcake, 260–63
orange buttercream frosting, 134–35, 221–23
Orange Cupcakes, Whole Wheat Cranberry, 54–55
Orange Icy Cupcake Pops, 218, 221–23, 226
Oreo cookie crumbles, 112, 114

pailletés, chocolate, 101
Pancake Medallions, Tiganites, 59, 60–61
paper baking cups, xxii–xxiii
pastries, 198–99
Peach Cupcakes, Ginger, 192–93
Peach Nectar Iced Tea, 197

Peanut Butter Chip Cupcakes, Chocolate, 206, 245–46
pearls, edible, 101
Peppermint Bark, Chocolate, 157–59
Peppermint Cupcakes, White Chocolate, 258–60
Phyllo Pastries, Pumpkin, 146–47
place cards, 22–23, 29
Pop Rocks Cupcakes, Chocolate Salted Caramel, 74–77
Pumpkin Phyllo Pastries, 146–47
punch, 139

raspberries, 28, 128–29, 139
Raspberry Buttercream "Tutu" Cupcakes, 12, 14–15
rose decorations, 38–41, 101, 112–15, 117
rum/rum extract, 154, 155

Salted Caramel Pop Rocks Cupcakes, Chocolate, 74–77
sanding sugar, 100
Sangria, 234
seating plans, 26
sesame seeds, 98–99, 122
Shortbread Valentine's Cookies, Strawberry, 84–85
Shortcake Cupcakes, Strawberry, 80–82
signature swirl, xxv
Spice Cupcakes, Greek Walnut, 266–67
spiderwebs, chocolate, 137
sports jersey fondant, 245–47
Star of David Blue Velvet Cupcakes, 164–65
strawberries, 13, 234
Strawberry Milk Shakes, 121
Strawberry Shortbread Valentine's Cookies, 84–85
Strawberry Shortcake Cupcakes, 80–82
sugar, sanding/crystallized, 100
sunflowers, frosting, 116
syrup, orange/lemon, 194

table setting, 148
Tarts, Cherry Cupcake, 236, 240–41
Tea, Peach Nectar Iced, 197

Teacake Cupcakes, Lavender Earl Grey, 24–25
teacup serving pieces, 181
tea sandwiches, 186–87
Tie-Dyed Monster Cupcakes, 136–38
Tiganites (Pancake Medallions), 59, 60–61
timelines, 149
Toasted Marshmallow Campfire Cupcakes, 214–16
toasting, 71
"Turkey" Cupcakes, Cranberry Spice, 144–45

vanilla
    buttercream frosting, 62–64, 122, 136–37, 224, 246, 247
    choosing, xxiii
    cream cheese frosting, 13, 144, 154–55, 164–65, 254
vanilla beans
    buying, 200–201
    recipes with, 80–82, 106, 121, 128–29, 182–83
vanilla creme filling, 80
vanilla ice cream, 121, 226
vanilla yogurt, in Marble Cupcakes, 44–45
Vasilopita (New Year's Cake), 70, 72–73
violets, 101, 117

walnuts, 194, 195
Walnut Spice Cupcakes, Greek, 266–67
wedding cupcake tower, 35
wedding favors, 36–37
whipped cream, 128
White Cheddar and Marmalade Tea Sandwiches, 187
White Chocolate Mini Egg Cupcakes, 94–96
White Chocolate Peppermint Cupcakes, 258–60
Whole Wheat Cranberry Orange Cupcakes, 54–55
Witches Brew, 139

Yellow Ducky Cupcakes, 62–65
Yogurt Cupcakes, Honeybee, 108, 112–15
Yogurt Parfaits, Cinnamon Cupcake and Honey, 194–95